Training for Endurance

Dr. Philip Maffetone's Guide
for Cyclists, Triathletes and Runners

Foreword by Mike Pigg

Introduction by Mark Allen

The information contained in this book is from the author's experiences and is not intended to replace medical advice. It is not the intent of the author to diagnose or prescribe. Before beginning any program you should consult with your physician, and address any questions to your physician.

Case studies in this book are real people whose names have been changed.

Printed in the United States of America

Library of Congress Catalog Number: 96-083504

ISBN 0-9642062-1-8

David Barmore Productions
P.O. Box 250
Stamford, NY 12167

For all who seek endurance
and optimal human performance.

Many have assisted in the preparation of this book. Special thanks goes to Matthew Fitzgerald for editing assistance, Ann Kim for production assistance and especially William Katovsky for his creative support. My appreciation also goes to Katharine Williams for her imaginative ideas. In addition, all the athletes I ever worked with taught me a great deal about training for endurance.

Table of Contents

Foreword
by Mike Pigg

Train slower to go faster? Is this guy a crazy or what? Phil Maffetone is not a crazy and I feel very fortunate to have met him when I did. I have been a professional triathlete since 1984. When I started my career, I just picked up the triathlon magazine to see what the top pros were doing and then just tried to emulate them. The one guy who was a star at the time was Scott Molina. He was doing mega miles in all three sports, plus doing speed workouts for each of the disciplines as if he was just a runner, cyclist or swimmer only. It looked like a good way to be the best, especially if you had the time to just eat, sleep, swim, bike and run. Things went well for me during the first three years. In 1988, I was able to work my way up to the top rank. I thought I was invincible. That is when the bumpy road started. I had no control over my progression. I was also starting to lose my love for the sport. It got so bad that I was about to quit and move on. The training became too hard and my results weren't there to justify the pain. That's about the time I ran into Phil.

We sat down and had a long talk. At first it was hard for me to swallow what Phil had to say. What helped me is that I have spent a lot of time training with Mark Allen. What I learned from Mark is that his heart rate was always lower than mine during long rides by 10 to 15 beats. During our long rides our pace would be even the first 65 miles than I would start a slow death out on the plains of Boulder, CO. I was like the hummingbird who needed fuel all the time and Mark was like a steam engine that you throw on the coals and cruise for hours and hours. Also, I was impressed by how consistent Mark's career was going with very few flaws year after year. Then the topper of it all was that Mark had been following Phil's plan already for many years.

So I listened to Phil with both ears wide open. After our conversation, Phil gave me one of his books. It was an easy reading book that had a lot of common sense about how to train and eat properly. So, I decided to follow the "180 Formula" and over a little time have become a firm believer in this aerobic heart rate training program.

The training seemed slow at first at my designated heart rate of 155. There were times when I had to walk up hills during the run and zig zag on the bike just to stay in my aerobic range. In a little time, things started to change and I became stronger at the same heart rate which became quite exciting. After 5 months of loyal training, I got my first big sign that the program was working.

Now, I have two stories of my own experience of following Phil's program for the last three years starting in 1993. Before going on the program, I would ride to my parents' summer place which is 65 miles with three good climbs in it. My previous record was set with a good friend of mine. We had the total grudge match all the way to find who was king of the bike. He would attack on the hills and I was holding a heart rate between 165 and 182 to establish a record of 3 hours and 15 minutes. When we arrived at the cabin I would achieve a total bonk. The best I could do for the rest of the day was eat, sleep and eat and even that was difficult. Three years later and 5 months on the aerobic program, I attempted the same course again. This time solo and never went above 155 even on the long climb. The results were interesting; I went 3:09 and felt good enough to go for a 10 mile run straight after. Slowly, I was becoming convinced that the theory was working.

My other story comes from the first race of the season while following Phil's plan. It is amazing how I was seeing good aerobic results in my workouts but still had doubts about my performance level. You see, I still needed my hammer sessions to prove to me or build my confidence that I was ready to race at a professional level. The season opener was in Australia at Surfers Paradise International Triathlon. My confidence was so blown that I didn't even want to get on the plane. But a swift kick from my wife and I was off. The whole week prior to the race, I was fighting myself, saying that I wasn't going to do well because of a lack of speed training. Finally, I told myself to shut up and go have a good time. To my surprise I did have a good time and won. For some reason the speed was there and my endurance definitely there. Plus a bonus, I was able to beat Mark Allen at his own game.

Now I am hooked. I am in love with my profession and staying healthy at the same time. Dr. Maffetone's guidelines are easy. All you need is a heart rate monitor to listen to your ticker and a little patience. And yes you can do it just by slowing down and letting your body catch up with your mind.

Best wishes,
Mike Pigg

Introduction
by Mark Allen

My athletic career started in 1968 when I answered an ad in the local paper announcing swim team tryouts. At the time I literally couldn't make it more than the length of a 25 yard pool without having to stop and catch my breath. In the nearly thirty years since, I have gone through almost every form of training theory and coaching style in the pursuit of my personal athletic excellence. The evolution to my present program was not easy. The years of regimented swim coaching had ingrained a very narrow-minded training philosophy into me, which was *do more faster*. If I could just train more yardage, and train faster, then I would most certainly race faster. Or so I thought.

My race results from this type of program were mediocre at best. *Do more faster* really only worked for those so talented that there genetics were going to override the lunacy of their training and take them to greatness anyway. I ended my 12-year swimming career completely burned out physically and mentally. I also ended it feeling like I just didn't reach my potential. But at the time, I couldn't put my finger on the answer as to why.

Fortunately, I was given a second chance to explore the limits of my athletic abilities. In 1982 I embarked on what has been a dream trip through the world of triathlons. It wasn't always smooth, though. My initiation years were a mirror to my swimming career. A few great results were separated by injuries and sporadic improvement, due specifically to the swimming mentality of *do more faster*. But unlike swimming, which is not an impact sport, the price of unwise training in triathlons is not only mental decay, but physical as well. Something needed to change.

Just about this time I was introduced to Phil Maffetone who had been having a lot of success training some local triathletes. I was warned that his methods were probably going to sound crazy at first, but that they really worked. That was 1984. And yes, at the time his philosophy on training was almost completely opposite from my swimming *do more faster* approach. It's 1996. And his once crazy sounding training techniques are almost universally accepted as the only way to train that will allow you to reach your peak performance year after year. Using Phil's training program and consulting with him over the years, I have been able to rack up a long list of international triathlon victories, including six Hawaiian Ironman titles, the last of which came at age thirty-seven!

In the pages that follow, Dr. Maffetone details the training philosophy that I have used throughout my triathlon career. If you have used these tools, you know they work. If you haven't, welcome to what will undoubtedly be a whole new level of athletic performance. Take the time to follow his program. Leave your ego at the door, because in the short term it might seem like you aren't going anywhere. But long term, I guarantee you will see the results you know your body is capable of.

See you at the races,

Mark Allen
Six-Time Ironman Champion and World Record Holder

Chapter 1

The Art & Science of Endurance

It was without conscious design that coaching (a word I'll use synonymous with trainer) became part of my professional career. My diverse athletic background included many coaches, most of whom trained me no different than the rest of the team. I recognized years ago that most coaching was done in this "cook book" fashion, with no individual considerations.

Once I entered private practice it became evident that coaching had to be part of caring for athletes. I was an applied kinesiologist; with the fortunate trait that I was able to understand the true sense of the word "holistic." And treating an athlete also meant extending that care into their lifestyle.

The most important aspect of this "total athlete" concept was assessment – getting feedback from the athlete. Not only conscious reactions of how the person was feeling, but more objective, measurable data which would assist both of us in developing an ideal training program from month to month, for years.

After beginning private practice in 1977, I quickly learned an important lesson in caring for the athletic patient. A local runner, Andy, came to see me with a leg injury. The problem seemed simple to correct, and he was out of pain after his second visit. But a month later, he returned with a similar symptom. I treated him again, and obtained equally good results. But several weeks later Andy returned with a different injury, a problem in the low back.

Although I evaluated Andy's diet and asked about other potential stress, one mistake I made was presuming he knew how to train. Although he understood the basics, he could not individualize his training to meet his particular needs. That is a difficult task for any of us to do properly.

Before I realized it was time to take a closer look at his training, Andy was gone. He sought relief from another doctor. Unfortunately, his journey from one professional to another continued for some time, as it had before me. While I lost track of his travels, he taught me a great lesson, one I previously could only conceptualize: look at the whole picture.

After my experience with Andy, I looked at every athlete's diary, and had them tell me in detail how they were training and racing. I realized that part of my treatment, if I was going to take a holistic view, had to include modifying the athlete's training schedule if necessary, to make it fit with everything else in their life.

For the endurance athlete, that is what I would like to share in this book: a view of the whole story, the big picture. Every aspect of your life affects all others. And if you want to succeed in your training and racing, a wide angle view is the best approach.

This is a book about my program for the endurance athlete. It combines experiences and observations, academic facts and theories of mine and others from many fields of health care and sports. The main focus is outcome: what works best for an individual athlete at a given point in their life. It is a program that combines both the art and science of training and racing.

But there are some ground rules that must be abided by. They are not my rules, but nature's. The first and most important is that what is done in training and racing be health promoting. In other words, it's not acceptable to sacrifice your health to get faster. If you do, you pay the penalty in the form of injury or ill health – somewhere down the road. This idea was obvious early in my career, and I set forth some basic definitions of health and fitness. I'll repeat them here because they are so important.

> *Health is defined as a state where all the body's systems are working in harmony. These include not just the muscle system, but the circulatory, skeletal, lymphatic, nervous and all other parts of the body.*

> *Fitness is the ability to be athletic. The more fit a person has become, the more effective they compete.*

Injuries, sickness, fatigue and other symptoms common to many athletes are indications of an imbalance between health and fitness. While these problems are common, they are not normal in endurance sports like they are in contact events. It is unfortunate that most athletes are willing, consciously or not, to sacrifice their health for more fitness.

While my program was developed for the typical endurance athlete, it assumes everyone is unique, with specific needs. Whether you are a reigning professional or a beginner, this program will work because you will be able to tailor it to fit your many needs.

The case histories in this book are real, with the names changed. They serve as real life examples, and demonstrate that your problems are often shared by many other endurance athletes. And more importantly, correction of these problems, along with prevention, is quite often easily managed.

As humans, we are all endurance athletes. Those of us who choose to develop our natural talents more fully and compete, must rely on training proficiency. But why can't we depend on intuition? I believe our instincts hold great powers. But allowing that sense to come out in a useful form, it must maneuver through our conscious mind. Here is where potential problems may exist. We have all grown up with many influences, positive and negative ones. Some have become our beliefs in the form of tradition. These attitudes, such as "no pain no gain" are well ingrained in our brains. Others are more subtly deposited, the result of media hype and advertising propaganda. These life-long recordings can easily cloud our natural instinct, making intuitive training very difficult. In time, however, by learning more about our body and its needs, training and racing by intuition can be our most effective technique. And it is a method we should all strive to achieve. In many ways, my program is a step toward that goal.

Chapter 2

Definitions for Modern Athletes

In endurance circles, trying to define common everyday words can result in a variety of meanings, sometimes dramatically. Ask a dozen seasoned endurance athletes what the word endurance means, and you're likely to get a dozen different definitions.

Part of the problem of defining endurance stems from the fact that this word can have many different meanings, depending on who you are. As a common term, Funk & Wagnall's New International Dictionary defines endurance as "the capacity or power to endure; ability to suffer pain, distress, hardship, or any very prolonged stress without succumbing; patient fortitude." But the 25th edition of Dorland's Medical Dictionary doesn't even list the word.

Even in academic circles, definitions can vary. In *Exercise Physiology,* McArdle defines endurance as "the time limit of a person's ability to maintain either a specific isometric force or a specific power level involving combination of concentric or eccentric muscular contractions." And in *Physiology of Sport and Exercise,* Wilmore and Costill describe it as "the ability to resist fatigue; includes muscular endurance and cardiorespiratory endurance." While these are important academic explanations, few endurance athletes and coaches can relate to them in practical, useful ways.

Without a common definition of endurance we all can relate to, interpreting the information in this book may be difficult. So allow me to propose a definition useful for the endurance field, one we can all relate to more in training and racing than in a laboratory.

My definition of endurance relates to athletes who engage in training at distances lasting more than about 5 to 15 minutes:

> *A steady state level of activity where one can develop and sustain relatively high speeds at submaximum effort over time; the ability to develop higher speeds while remaining predominantly aerobic; increasing the percent fat burning and decreasing the dependence on carbohydrate utilization with training.*

An important aspect of endurance is that it should not only persist for many years, but improve annually; with a peak not being reached until well into the fourth decade of life.

Obviously, I don't include sprinters in this category of endurance athletes. They have some similar needs and may benefit greatly by following many of the techniques and philosophies described in this book.

Some humans possess great sprinting ability. By sprinting, I refer to the very short activity lasting only a few seconds to less than a minute. One unique difference between sprinters and endurance athletes is genetics. Bouchard and his colleagues at Laval University in Quebec City have shown in research what many coaches have known for years; that sprinters are born and endurance athletes are made. He concluded that the anaerobic power found in world class sprinters, like Carl Lewis, is 92% inherited, while endurance champions inherit only 25% of their ability, with the remainder coming through training.

Endurance athletes include triathletes and duathletes, road runners and cyclists, mountain bikers, swimmers, skaters and cross country skiers. But others not usually thought of as endurance athletes must possess endurance ability or they will succumb to injury and short athletic lifespans. These include basketball, hockey, football, soccer and baseball players, and even race car drivers.

Endurance sports, in both natural and organized forms, has existed for centuries. But as an established class, today's endurance athletes, by far the largest of the two groups, have been influenced more by sprinters than by distance coaches, athletes and others.

Case History
Larry was a great sprinter in high school and college, performing well in the 100 and 200 meter, the long jump and short indoor distances too. Now a 37 year-old endurance athlete, his training program still included track workouts from spring through early winter. On the track he would perform sprint drills, do 200, 400 and 800 meter repeats and occasionally a 5K time trial. But Larry was often injured and his 5K time trials were often better than his races for the same distance.

When I began working with Larry, he had a difficult time with a schedule that did not include sprint workouts. But he was delighted with the results, which included being injury free and personal bests. He finally realized that performing on the roads was really a different sport than what he did in his early track days.

As the running, cycling and triathlon boom evolved, influential personalities, especially coaches and well known athletes from track and field and other sprint sports including swimming and biking, emerged too. As a result of their presence and their training techniques, the trend of training like a sprinter was maintained. As a result, today's endurance athletes often hold on to that tradition of sprint workouts – track, road or pool intervals – to increase speed.

If we look at the time commitment associated with these anaerobic benefits, and weigh them against the benefits in competition, we get a better picture. For example, in a one-hour event only 2% of our energy comes from the anaerobic system. In a two-hour event only 1% of our energy is derived from anaerobic sources. Does it make sense to spend so many hours a week on anaerobic work when 99% of our race is aerobic?

As I will discuss in detail in later chapters, we should derive most of our speed from aerobic training. But before moving on to these other topics, more definitions are necessary. Two important ones are the terms aerobic and anaerobic.

Take a snapshot of the body's metabolism, and the most obvious feature is oxygen. As everyone knows, oxygen is essential for energy production. But not all energy is obtained with the help of oxygen. We can get energy from reactions that require oxygen, and energy that does not need oxygen. When oxygen is used to generate energy, it is called aerobic, and when the body derives energy without using oxygen it is termed anaerobic. This is the common way athletes and coaches look at these definitions.

However, this scheme refers to the conversion sugar or glucose. In reality, sugar (originating mostly from dietary carbohydrates) is only one of two main sources of energy. The other is fat.

Depending on a person's training and nutrition, 80 to 90% of their total energy can be derived from fat. The conversion of fat to energy takes place in the slow-twitch or red muscle fibers. These are also referred to as aerobic muscle fibers. These muscle fibers are used during longer, relatively slower activity lasting 5 to 15 minutes or more. When an endurance athlete fatigues in a race, it is due to the loss of available glucose necessary to sustain the conversion of fat to energy in the aerobic muscle fiber.

The specific muscle fiber where glucose is converted to energy is the fast-twitch or white muscle fiber, also referred to as the anaerobic muscle fiber. These muscle fibers are used for short distance speed, since anaerobic energy is very limited to one to three minutes.

Classic definitions of aerobic and anaerobic relate to either the need for oxygen, or its absence. But it does not take into account the source of the energy – sugar or fat – which is a distinguishing feature, or the muscle fibers which not only converts sugar or fat to energy, but propels the athlete during training and racing.

I propose a definition of aerobic and anaerobic based on both the source of energy and the type of muscle fiber used. Relating aerobic and anaerobic this way to training and racing makes it a more simple, complete and useful definition.

Aerobic: The ability of the body to use more fats and less sugar (glucose) for energy;

Anaerobic: The ability of the body to use more sugar (glucose) and less fat for energy;

While we separate specific aspects of the body in the ways described above for convenience, the truth is all components of the body work together in harmony. For example, we nearly always use both glucose and fat for energy, and both aerobic and anaerobic muscle fibers during endurance activity.

We see this harmony best when measuring the amount of glucose and fat the body is using at a given intensity during training. The respiratory quotient (RQ) or respiratory exchange ratio (RER) is the amount of carbon dioxide exhaled divided by the oxygen consumed. From this number it is possible to obtain a fairly accurate percentage of glucose and fat used for energy. For example, a ratio of .85 indicates that about half the energy used is derived from glucose, and half from fats.

As endurance improves, so does the use of fats for energy. This fat burning may increase to 50, 60 or 70% or more at submaximum intensities. In disciplined athletes, tremendous values for fat burning have been obtained. The following chart was compiled on triathlete Mike Pigg:

Heart Rate	RQ	%Fat	%Sugar
127	.79	70	30
133	.80	67	33
135	.82	60	40
137	.83	56	44
141	.84	53	47
146	.82	60	40
153	.85	50	50
153	.85	50	50
155*	.87	42	58
164	.87	42	58
169	.90	32	68

*At 155 heart rate, Mike can run sub-5:25 pace.

This brief introduction to aerobic and anaerobic metabolism is only the tip of a very large and complex iceberg. My definition of aerobic and anaerobic has been simplified and made more useful for endurance athletes and not necessarily for the professional doing laboratory research. More importantly, it is a practical way to relate to training and racing, as we will see.

Even more useful are some simple definitions of the word training. Although this explanation is in the form of an equation, it is very important to always remember it:

Training = Work + Rest

More specifically, work is your workout; the daily training routine which builds muscles, improves their efficiency, increases oxygen uptake, etc. In physiology it's called overload. In the case of a muscle, you must work it slightly harder than it is used to in order to rebuild and improve its function.

But work is not limited to your training. It can also mean house, yard or office work, taking care of the kids, shopping, etc. This activity still burns fat and sugar, works the muscles, stimulates the metabolism and nervous system. Although it won't necessarily help you in training, it must be considered because it is still work and you must recover from it.

An important part of the equation is rest. It is during this rest phase that your body recovers from training. It allows your muscles and other working parts to re-build and prepare for the next bout of training. During this phase, there should be no work, and sufficient sleep. But if you have to work, shop or take care of the kids, you not resting as much as you can. Since most athletes don't have the luxury of complete rest, care must be taken to avoid training beyond one's ability to recover from it. For most, that means cut down on training to keep the equation balanced.

If you don't provide enough rest, your body will not be ready for more work. Or, if you work beyond the muscle's or body's ability to rest, or recover from the workload, you overtrain. Any of these imbalances can result in a series of malfunctions which may cause injury, ill health or burn out.

For most athletes the work part of the equation is actually the easy aspect of training. It is the rest phase that is most often difficult and neglected.

Case history
Bob was a good local runner who desperately wanted to improve. But his expanding business and growing family was demanding more time from his busy training schedule. He tried to accommodate everyone and maintain his training. He woke up early every morning to get in his daily run. Within a few months he was exhausted and began feeling pain in his knees and back. In the middle of a very successful racing season, his times began to deteriorate. The first thing I recommended when Bob consulted me was to cut his training down by about 40%, since he was not able to decrease any of his other commitments. Almost immediately his energy improved and his physical problems disappeared. After about 4 weeks on his modified schedule, Bob ran a great race, and continued racing well for the rest of the season.

If you work a full time job, have a family, a house or all of the above, you're busy. You can still workout and train successfully if you balance the equation. Of all the endurance athletes I initially see, most are working out far more than necessary. Even today, I spend a lot of time convincing ath-

letes to cut down. When they do, they feel better, work out more efficiently and their performance improves.

Definitions should be useful for those who are involved in the process.
Keeping the definitions of endurance, training, aerobic and anaerobic both
simple and practical helps everyone understand the bigger picture.

Chapter 3

Athletes & Stress

Excess stress is not only the most common problem I see in athletes, but the most neglected and underestimated by them. Stress is such an important aspect of, and influence on training that I include it early in this book. Understanding what stress is will help you more effectively manage and avoid it. And that will immensely assist in your effort to get healthy and fit.

Stress can be defined as any factor that effects the body (or mind) which causes the body to react and adapt. This reaction and adaptation is managed to a large extent by the adrenal glands, located on top of each kidney. These glands are also responsible for recovery from the stress of training. The response to stress takes time and energy, with more stress requiring more time and energy to properly adapt.

Stress can come from anywhere; your job, family, other people. It comes in the form of severe emotions, infections, allergic reactions, physical trauma and exertion, the weather. But not all stress is negative. Since stress is a factor that evokes a reaction in the body, the outcome may also be positive one. Your workout is an example. By stressing your muscles and metabolism, the end result over time is that your body performs better. But that same stressor – your workout – can turn to a negative if you go too far beyond the body's ability to recover.

We can categorize stress on three levels: physical, chemical and mental. Physical stress includes your workout, bodily strain at your job site, such as sitting at a desk all day, prolonged driving in a car or truck, or heavy lifting. Wearing improper training shoes or riding a bike not set up right for your body are also common physical stresses.

Chemical stress can adversely effect the body too. Improper nutrition, dehydration, and too much caffeine are typical examples. Body chemistry controls most bodily functions, including the nervous system and brain, muscles and the intestines. So these areas are especially sensitive to chemical stress.

Most people think of stress in its mental form. Tension, anxiety and depression are common examples. But unrealistic athletic goals, not understanding or having knowledge about even simple things like your bike set up or airline travel tension are also familiar stresses.

More often people have stress from more than one category; and frequently from a combination of all three types. And, stress is cumulative. The response to a physical stress from a Sunday race may be amplified by a chemical stress on Monday and further compounded with a mental stress on Tuesday. All of which will effect your training on Wednesday through Friday, and finally your Saturday race.

The weather is also a potential stressor, with certain people more vulnerable. Weather stress may effect us physically, chemically or mentally. Extremes in temperatures or humidity, very low barometric pressure, and the sun are illustrations. Because of weather stress, training or racing in these environments usually has adverse effects on your body and performance.

One distinguishing feature of many top athletes is their ability to tolerate stress. A small part of this coping mechanism of the adrenal glands may be genetic. But those without strong adrenals still have an option; stress control. The key to controlling stress is to first carefully assess it, with the goal of diminishing or eliminating some of your stress. The first step is to make a list of all your stress, taking several days to complete it (you won't think of all your different stresses right away). Then separate that list into two parts. Make the "A" list from stress you can eliminate or control. This may include unhealthy eating habits like rushing your meals, to trying to get a few more miles out of your already worn out shoes. The "B" list is comprised of stress you can't control very well. This may include job stress or the weather. In reality, almost any stress can be modified or eliminated. It's a question of how far you want to go to eliminate stress.

Once you can "see" your stress on paper, it will be easier to manage. Start with your "A" list stresses first because you have control over them – not that it's always easy. You may be able to improve on some and totally eliminate others. Some will require habit changes. In all, it's a big task, but one that will return great benefits.

Then there's the "B" list of stress; if there's nothing you can do about them anyway, don't worry about them. By regulating the stress on your "A" list, your adrenal glands will have a much easier time managing the ones on your "B" list.

In addition to making your stress lists, you're probably familiar with other strategies for dealing with stress. But for many of you, most of the time you don't use them. Here's a reminder of some of them:

- Just say "no" when asked to do something you really don't want to do.
- Decide not to waste your present time over the past, or worry about the future. (That's not to say you should ignore the past or not plan for the future.)
- Learn some relaxation techniques, and perform them regularly.
- When you're concerned about something, or when a problem comes up, talk it over with someone you trust.
- Simplify your life. Start by eliminating trivia.
- Prioritize your busy schedule; do the most important things first.

What's most important about stress is that too much of it interferes with rest. Or more accurately, excess stress requires more rest. And if you don't have enough rest, your training is adversely affected. In many ways, stress is also like work. Here again, too much stress, like work, interferes with training.

Case History
Janet owned a business, had a family and was a triathlete. Fitting all three sports into her schedule was always more of a challenge than her races. She complained that stress was her main problem but brushed it aside saying it was part of life. For Janet, listing all her stress on paper was a frightening experience, but a revelation. Janet was able to eliminate and modify many little problems from her day. Over the next few months, she got her kids to do more of the work at home, hired a new office manager, and did many workouts around her time instead of everyone else's. Eventually, Janet not only felt better, but her performances improved too.

A common stress, a mental one, is obsession. I'm not talking about compulsive disorders or other more obvious and extreme problems, but the common obsessions many of us harbor. Too often, these "mental fixations" over-run our rational mind when it comes to training. A frequent example may be your Sunday workout with a group of athletes. You go out the door for an easy workout but without a real training plan, and follow the group. But it usually turns out to be an obsessive race rather than the intended easy workout. Or, you complete a long hard race and a few days later you're asked to go for a long run with the group. You feel good and are almost obligated to go – and train too hard.

Another trademark of obsession is the fear that taking a day off will ruin all your training. Or somehow, you will lose benefits previously gained. This is often the case during a taper before a long race, and the days and weeks following a long hard effort.

Counting miles is another common obsession. At the end of your training week you tally up 38 miles; so you run two extras just to get to 40, despite feeling tired. Or you jog the 80 meters from your car to the office twice daily and include that in your weekly mileage.

All these obsessions are significant stresses and can adversely effect your training, racing and health.

Since stress is regulated by the adrenal glands, high levels of stress keeps your adrenals quite busy. This is a very significant aspect of training when you consider the other work your adrenals have to do.

The adrenal glands not only regulate stress, improve endurance and racing but they are essential for life. These benefits are obtained through the action of hormones produced by the adrenals.

The glucocorticoids, which include cortisol, are an important group of adrenal hormones with several actions. They have anti-inflammatory actions, which you need on a daily basis if you train. Even an easy workout can produce some inflammation from wear and tear. Without the adrenal's control over this process, the inflammation would persist, ultimately preventing you from training. Cortisol also helps make fat more available for energy, sparing glucose in the process, and it stimulates protein utilization necessary for repair and recovery.

The mineralocorticoids help regulate our electrolytes, especially sodium and potassium. Aldosterone, the main mineralocorticoid, keeps sodium in the body. In this process, water levels are more easily maintained which counters the potential for dehydration.

Epinephrine and norepinephrine are two other important adrenal hormones. They increase the rate and power of the heartbeat, increase metabolism, and help release sugar and fat for energy use. These hormones also improve circulation in the working muscles, partly by increasing blood pressure, and increase respiration.

Many of the adrenal hormones increase with training intensity. But too much adrenal activity can pose a problem. For example, too much cortisol suppresses the immune system. One symptom of overtraining is a lowered body defense mechanism.

Table 1
Some important adrenal hormones and their actions

Hormone	Action
Glucocorticoids	Anti inflammatory, increases fat burning, spares glucose, promotes protein use.
Mineralcorticoids	Regulates electrolytes and water.
Epinephrine and Norepinephrine	Improves blood flow to muscles, promotes fat and glucose use.

Adrenal activity functions like clockwork, and is referred to as your circadian rhythm. A change in time zones, which may take place when you fly east or west, produces stress with more produced with larger changes in time. The common symptom of "jet lag" results. You stay on your previous time schedule until the adrenal glands adapt to the stress, which may take several days depending on how far off schedule you are. If you've ever competed several time zones away without first adapting, you probably understand this example of how stress works.

In the early part of this century a young medical student named Hans Selye began to piece together the common triad of signs resulting from excess adrenal stress. They include adrenal gland enlargement, depressed immunity and intestinal dysfunction. Selye eventually showed how the adrenals react to stress when confronted with an excess of it. This *General Adaptation Syndrome* has three distinct stages.

The three stages of adrenal reaction to stress begin with the alarm reaction, in which there is an increase in adrenal hormone production. This is an attempt by the adrenals to battle the increased stress. If it is successful, adrenal function returns to normal. But if over time the adrenals fail to meet the needs of the body to combat the stress, the adrenals enter the second phase called the resistance stage.

During this period, the adrenal gland itself get larger; a process called hypertrophy. Since the increased hormone production could not counter the stress, the body decides to enlarge the whole gland as an attempt to do the same. If the stress is still not controlled, the adrenals enter the third stage, simple called exhaustion.

The exhaustion stage is just that; exhaustion. The adrenal gland is unable to adapt to stress. It has lost the war. As an endurance athlete, if you are in the exhaustion stage you may be considering retirement from racing and maybe even from training, or at best feeling quite bad and are struggling to figure out what's wrong. Maybe some well meaning professional has given you a fancy name of a symptom, the end result of adrenal exhaustion, which somehow makes you feel a bit at ease, having a name for what you feel.

In this exhaustion stage, the adrenals are unable to effectively counter the stress placed upon it. At this point, the person usually becomes symptomatic – anything from physical and mental exhaustion to chronic injuries, from immune system dysfunction and ulcers to other more serious health problems.

The General Adaptation Syndrome may take weeks, months or even years to build. As stated earlier, stress is cumulative. So unless the body can adapt well, adrenal stress can worsen over the years. Early symptoms commonly include fatigue and recurrent injuries, especially knee, low back and foot problems. Also, dizziness upon standing, low blood pressure and allergies are typical.

Table 2
The Body's Reaction to Stress: The General Adaptation Syndrome

1. alarm reaction: increased adrenal hormone production

2. resistance stage: enlargement of the adrenal gland

3. exhaustion stage: adrenal glands unable to adapt to stress

In my practice, excess adrenal stress – or a lack of the adrenals to adapt to stress – is one of the most common problems found in endurance athletes. It may be due to overtraining, poor diet, work or family stress, or as is most often the case, a combination of stress which has cumulated.

The remedy for stress, as discussed above, is to look at your stress, eliminate those that can be disposed of, and if possible modify as many of the others as possible. One of the items easily modified is training. This is the reason why cutting down on workouts in time and intensity often improves performance: by lowering your stress levels the adrenal glands can "catch up" and your health and fitness improves.

Causes of stress and their remedies can vary significantly, as it is a very individual problem. Evaluating your physical stress is a good start. Are your training shoes in good shape? Do you slouch when sitting?

Chemically, various nutrients are sometimes required when there is excess stress since the adrenals utilize these to function. Vitamins B–6, C and pantothenic acid, and the mineral zinc are common examples. An over-consumption of refined sugar or large amounts of caffeine are frequent excesses which can add a burden to the adrenal glands.

Mental tension about anything, or everything, is counterproductive for the adrenal glands. Meditation, whether done formally in a quiet location or informally when training by yourself is often very helpful.

Whatever the problem, the cause of the excess adrenal stress, or why the glands could not counter existing stress, must be found and corrected. If you are successful, the body's natural endurance ability will be released and often progresses dramatically.

Case History
Michael loved to run, but had chronic knee and low back pain, allergies and intestinal problems which always interfered with his racing plans. He also had insomnia and could not get the rest he needed. He was a textbook case of a stressed athlete with matching symptoms. His diet revealed a large amount of sugar consumption, about 9 cups of coffee a day and no breakfast. And, he worked about 60 hours a week in a very physical job.

Michael wanted to qualify for the Boston Marathon. But my concern was for his overall health. His blood pressure and cholesterol were too high, and his weight and body fat were increasing each year. In the next 12 months, Michael successfully improved his health by eliminating coffee and sugar, eating a healthy diet and restricting his training. A year later he qualified for Boston and ran a 2:54 Marathon.

Stress Testing

Traditionally, stress testing is a screening procedure used to evaluate the heart under the tension of exercise. Most tests are done on treadmills, with bicycle ergometers and step tests used about 30% of the time.

Stress tests, when indicated, are done following a general evaluation that includes blood tests and an electrocardiogram (ECG). However, about 30% of those with normal ECG's have heart disease. Of these, only 80% can be diagnosed from a stress test.

One benefit of a stress test is that it may uncover a hidden hypertension in someone who has normal blood pressure at rest.

The American College of Sports Medicine's standard for those individuals who should be stress tested includes a person under the age of 35 with evidence of heart disease or a significant combination of risk factors. Primary risk factors include hypertension, hyperlipidemia and cigarette smoking. Secondary risk factors include family history, obesity, diabetes mellitus.

It is generally not recommended that those under the age of 35 with no history or significant risk factors have a stress test.

Unfortunately, for most individuals with heart disease the most common first sign is death. And no one is immune, even athletes. But most risk factors are controllable, or at least easy to evaluate. Most athletes don't smoke, are active, and not obese. These are three significant risk factors. Simple blood tests for total cholesterol (with HDL and LDL) and triglycerides can rule out hyperlipidemia, and blood glucose can rule out diabetes mellitus. Having a professional check your blood pressure occasionally can also help rule out hypertension.

Even endurance athletes who train regularly should pay attention to any signs or symptoms of possible heart disease. Thirty percent of the initial manifestation of heart disease is accompanied by angina pectoris. This pain is usually in the upper chest but often is displayed in the left shoulder or arm, neck and jaw. The cause is due to a low level of blood and oxygen through the coronary artery, the main blood vessel of the heart. The symptom usually begins during activity and subsides with rest.

Stress tests are also not highly accurate. About 25% of tests are false-negative, meaning the test results have not uncovered an existing problem. In 15% of tests, there is a false-positives meaning it indicated a problem which does not exist; this leaves 60% of the tests accurate.

Chapter 4

The Practical Science of Training

No one really knows everything about endurance training. While science has come a long way, we still understand only a small piece of the big puzzle. But we are not lost between the hypothetical ideals of the perfect intuitive athlete and the flawlessly engineered scientific specimen. There can be logic in training, along with intuition. It is here that both art and science come together.

In this chapter, I would like to explore the scientific aspect of training, specifically the mechanisms influenced when we train, and how training in turn effects the body. It is these mechanisms which give us back what we ask for in health and performance.

When viewing the science of training, understand that all that is known is not black and white. Scientists continually debate many aspects of this field, and just as many attitudes, theories and facts are changed over time due to new research and observations. My point here is that science as we know it is not an exact science. And, the view you get here is mine. My academic background is very extensive, and much of my day is spent in textbooks and journal articles. But if the scientific aspect of training presented here is not relative and interesting, and simplified, you will soon be asleep.

The attempt is to make compatible the science and the clinical observations made in the athletes I work with. In many ways, they are my experiments. Through the trial and error process, we all learn how to succeed in sports, and how to obtain a healthier body and mind.

In a sense, there are several bodies within us, each representing different aspects of our physiology. When we train, these different parts are programmed to work in a very specific way. But what you ask your body to learn in training is not always what you really want it to do. An example of this in the development of speed. Old wisdom tells us if we want to race fast, we have to train fast. In one sense that seems logical. But in endurance sports what we get from training fast, like a sprinter, is not acceptable. The result is we obtain speed meant for a sprinter – short term and short lived. If we try and apply that to endurance activity, we run the risk of overtraining. While we all have an obsession for speed, this does not fit the definition of, or the desire for endurance. The different bodies within us which must be trained for endurance include the muscles, metabolism and the nerves.

Your workout trains the muscles, which are obviously vital in any athletic action. But they react only when, and how the nervous systems tells them to do so. That same workout also influences the nerves that attach to the muscles, while at the same time other parts of the nervous system effect the metabolism. Our energy is provided for by the metabolism so the muscles can perform. Each aspect of the body is in constant interaction with all the others, and what we do in training has significant influence over the whole body.

Let's take a closer look at these aspects of the body, the nervous system, the metabolism and the muscles, and see how each is intricately related to training.

Training the Nervous System
Perhaps the most important part of your body, the one most responsive to training and most important for competition, is the nervous system. All physiological activity is influenced by this system. In many ways, when we talk about training, we're referring to the neurological mechanisms.

Picture a large house with hundreds of meters of wires, some very thin, some large cables, all connecting together and controlled from a central switch box. The nervous system runs through your body in a similar way. Except it goes to every square millimeter of the body, and sends information both ways. The main processing center of the nervous system is the brain and spinal cord housed within our spines.

A good illustration of the nervous system's interrelationships throughout the body is its connection to the muscles. Each aerobic muscle fiber has a separate nerve connecting to it. The same is true with the anaerobic fibers. And that type of nerve fiber has a specific action much like the muscle fiber itself. For example, the nerve fiber attaching to the slow-twitch aerobic fiber is slower acting compared to the nerve fiber which joins the fast-twitch anaerobic muscle fiber, which is faster acting.

Training the slower nerves to stimulate their specific aerobic fibers – which work at submaximal efforts – is one key to building successful endurance. But this does not mean you will always be "slow" – the biggest fear all athletes have. In time, and with successful training, the slow-twitch aerobic muscles improve function and increase their speed, but still functioning as a slow twitch fiber.

If we don't train these specific parts of the nervous system, along with their connections with the aerobic muscles, and as many as possible, we never "learn" to build high quality aerobic activity. In training circles this is called building an aerobic base. In neurological terms, it is referred to as an engram, which are stored memories in the brain.

One unique ability of the nervous system is its capacity to learn. We've all experienced it. Leaning how to type, play the piano or perform any skill we learn by practice is the result of implanting memory into the nervous system. In the same way, training for endurance is no different. Each workout is a small part of a memory stored in the brain.

If we train indiscriminately, that is recorded. If we overtrain, that too is registered. But if we train effectively, we maintain that memory too. The nervous system remembers everything it experiences, so be careful what you put into it. Sometimes a long process of "re-training" is necessary, especially in those who have abused their body through improper training.

We can train our nervous system to function efficiently at a high endurance level. In order to do that, we have to influence the nerves that attach to the aerobic muscles. But we have to stimulate all of them, beginning with the smallest aerobic fibers, which move us very slow. Over time, as these nerves and muscles are trained, they work more efficiently. The result is they can do more work with the same effort. This translates into more speed from muscles and nerves that once were much slower.

The importance of the nervous system is exemplified in its influence on the muscle's power. Everyone thinks that the anaerobic muscles are more powerful in their actions than the slower moving aerobic ones. But this is untrue. Aerobic and anaerobic muscle fibers can generate the same potential force. The difference between them is neurological. When the nervous system calls for anaerobic action, more muscle fibers are activated into action by nerves compared to the same stimulation of aerobic muscles.

Training the Muscles
For most endurance athletes, too much focus in training is on the muscles. If they were the primary element in endurance, then weight lifting would provide more success than any other training technique. But the muscles

are just pawns in the endurance game. They are the work horses. And if we drive them too hard or not enough, we get less performance. However, the muscles still play an important role in endurance.

The aerobic muscle fibers are uniquely different from their anaerobic counterparts. Aerobic fibers are sometimes called "red" because they contain structures called mitochondria which contain the iron-protein compound myoglobin. It is here, through myoglobin action in the mitochondria, that oxygen is successfully used in the energy generating process. The more these muscle fibers are trained, the more mitochondria and myoglobin is created, and the more oxygen will be utilized to help produce energy. The mitochondria is also the site of fat burning.

Also unique to the aerobic muscle fiber is that it is generally fatigue resistant. Over time aerobic fatigue is due to the nervous and metabolic aspects as discussed below. Even after 10 hours of racing, there is still unused glycogen in the anaerobic fibers – unless you used it inadvertently during the event. If this small reserve is still intact, it is quite useful for your final kick.

Another important characteristic of the aerobic fiber is it's high concentration of blood vessels. Arteries bring blood into the fiber, along with oxygen and nutrients, including vitamins, minerals and fats. The veins bring blood out, carrying by-products such as carbon dioxide and lactic acid. These substances must be removed as quick as possible since they have the potential to slow the muscle's action.

Through endurance training you should develop much more circulation then would normally be possible. When aerobic fibers are left untrained, their potential blood vessels are also left unused. Transport of oxygen to the muscles is one of the limiting factors in performance.

Training all the aerobic muscle fibers allows us the use of the full spectrum of muscle we have – from the smallest walking fibers to the relatively fast aerobic ones. By doing that, we increase circulation, improve oxygen utilization, burn more fat, remove more by-products, and function more efficiently.

The aerobic fibers are the most commonly contracted part of the muscle, even in everyday action. Your physical activity at work and home, shopping and doing everyday chores requires aerobic muscle activity. This is where the potential risk of overtraining is of concern, not from your work-out but from all other activity you do in the course of the normal day or week. The sum of all your activity must be balanced if you are to get max-imum training benefits and avoid overtraining.

Endurance training should involve the use of as many aerobic fibers as possible. In doing so, we can't help using some of the anaerobic fibers. But the predominance will be in training the aerobic muscles. Even walk-ing, which activates the very slow moving aerobic fibers, has a place in endurance training. Especially for the professional.

The anaerobic muscles are our sprinting, power fibers, and are generally much larger than the aerobic ones. The anaerobic fibers are actually made up of three different kinds. The scientific terminology varies dramatically, but I will simply refer the anaerobic fibers as a, b and c types.

The type "a" fibers are really a combination of aerobic and anaerobic quality. These fibers are very important in endurance training and racing. Developing their aerobic quality further improves endurance, and most especially aerobic speed. When these fibers are highly developed, they are a lot like an aerobic fiber.

The type "b" fibers are the pure anaerobic types. They are made for power and short bursts of speed, but can only function for a very brief period of time – perhaps 2 to 3 minutes or less. These fibers rely exclusively on sugar for energy. The main reason their function is so short term is both glucose and glycogen are very limited.

Not nearly as much is known about the type "c" anaerobic fibers. It is found only in small numbers within the anaerobic population of fibers.

All muscles in the human body contain all the fibers mentioned above. They are assembled side by side each other in an almost random order. The different fibers are used when required. For example, during walking almost all the muscle action is from aerobic fibers. If you walk faster, more aerobic muscle is enlisted. Begin to jog and the "a" type anaerobic fibers are added into action, and as you increase your speed to higher intensity, more "b" type anaerobic fibers take over. But with faster activi-ty the slower moving aerobic fibers cease their action.

In some animals, like a chicken, different muscles have more exclusively certain fiber types. For example, the chicken's legs contains mostly aerobic muscle fibers; they are used for slow, constant walking. The "breast," however, is comprised of mostly anaerobic fibers – the white meat – used for fast, powerful but short lived flapping of the wings.

The percentage of different fibers in a given muscle varies between people. Certain muscles of elite endurance athletes contain up to 90% aerobic fibers, where sprinters may have as little as 25%, with the remainder being anaerobic. But remember that the anaerobic type "a" has significant aerobic function, so simply counting aerobic and anaerobic fibers can be misleading when relating to overall function. It is my opinion that some of the great sprinters can be trained to make great endurance athletes.

Knowing the percentage of aerobic and anaerobic muscle fibers, however, will do little in ascertaining that person's performance outcome. This is because the muscle itself is not the determining factor in performance, but the sum of the neurological, muscular and metabolic activity and efficiency.

In endurance athletes, the training effect more than makes up for any individual difference in fiber type, and genetics. While our particular fiber make-up is mostly genetically determined, our training determines the efficiency of those fibers. Also, some interesting changes may occur in training.

Can aerobic fibers be trained to change to anaerobic fibers, or vice versa? There is considerable controversy over whether fiber types can switch as a result of training. My personal opinion is they can.

Studies show that anaerobic training decreases the number of aerobic fibers and increases the number of type "c" anaerobic fibers. With aerobic training, there is an increase in the number of aerobic fibers. Another study showed similar results: a 23% increase in anaerobic fibers and the same percent decrease in aerobic fibers with only six weeks of sprint training. Inactivity, or detraining, may also decrease aerobic fiber percentages.

In addition, with age we lose some of our anaerobic fibers which results in a higher percentage of aerobic fibers in each muscle. This is one main reason why sprinters reach their peak early in life, and endurance athletes don't peak until the third or fourth decade, and can still continue performing at high levels for many years beyond that time.

As we all have experienced, muscles ultimately fatigue in the course of endurance activity. But it is not the muscle itself which tires, it's usually a combination of the neurological aspects we discussed above and the metabolic factors addressed below.

Over time in training or racing, there is a slowing and finally a cessation of nerve transmission to the muscle. The reasons for this are unknown. Metabolically, the muscle can run out of fuel (sugar and fat) even if enough oxygen and neurological stimulation is present. (In short sprints, fatigue occurs from a lack of oxygen.) This is usually the result of using up too much sugar by training or racing too hard.

Metabolic Training
Endurance training and competition requires moderate amounts of energy over long periods of time. This is different from sprinters who use very large amounts of energy in a very short period. But the energy used for every action has a long journey before we can access it.

All energy used for training and racing originates as light energy from the sun. Plants take in this energy, convert it and store it as chemical energy. We consume the plants or eat animals who feed on plants. The energy is transferred to us in the form of carbohydrates, proteins and fats, and we use it as mechanical energy.

Converting the foods we eat into usable energy for muscle action is the job of our metabolism. The quality of the food eaten and the efficiency of metabolism helps produce energy for training and performance.

Carbohydrates, proteins and fats are eaten and chemically broken down in the intestine and absorbed as glucose, amino acids and small fat particles. These food products are gradually separated into smaller chemicals. Eventually, on a molecular level, adenosine triphosphate, ATP, is produced. The ATP from food is used as energy for all biological work.

Three different methods of harnessing energy exist in our body. They are referred to as the CP, anaerobic and aerobic systems.

The CP system, creatine phosphate, is our most immediate energy source. The energy produced in this system is very limited. For example, at the beginning of a 100 meter sprint, an athlete may use CP for some of his energy. The CP system only has about 5 to 10 seconds worth of energy. This system will only be mentioned here, because it is emphasized less and its benefits minimized in endurance training relative to the other two systems.

For energy to be maintained beyond the time limits of the creatine phosphate, the anaerobic system is utilized. Energy from this system is derived from glucose in the anaerobic muscle fiber. Ideally, this energy system is most useful at the end of endurance competition, where a final kick is needed. But the maximum amount of energy the anaerobic system can generate is about three minutes worth of all out effort. If we use up this energy too early in competition, we adversely and sometimes tragically effect performance.

As we all know, a unique feature of the anaerobic system is that the process of energy production also generates lactic acid. As we mentioned earlier, there is always some anaerobic muscle activity, so there is a constant production of lactic acid in the anaerobic muscle. At rest and during submaximal activity, the small amount of lactic acid produced is eliminated quickly. It is only at high intensities that it accumulates. (Lactic acid is transported to the blood where it is chemically changed and called blood lactate.) In part, this accumulation of lactic acid restricts our performance.

With intense training and competition, most endurance athletes race with levels of blood lactate that are higher than resting, often significantly. Actually, race pace is limited to a great extent by the accumulation of blood lactate. This increase in lactic acid can be controlled best if the body has substantial aerobic muscle fiber development. In general, the better your aerobic base, the less lactate is produced. Removal of lactic acid is also more efficient when the blood circulation is more developed, which coincides with aerobic muscle fiber improvement. Even neighboring aerobic muscle fibers which are inactive during more intense activity are capable of eliminating or oxidizing lactic acid.

The blood lactate level is a very accurate predictor of performance and a successful way to monitor training quality. Studies using endurance athletes show that the race times were highly correlated with blood lactate. Evaluating max VO_2 is not only a poor predictor of actual performance but an ineffective indicator of training efficiency.

In general, blood lactate levels returns to normal resting levels within about 20 minutes after training or racing. The feeling of muscle soreness following activity is most likely due to the normal wear and tear on the muscle fibers.

Since the body has strict limitations on energy gained from the anaerobic system, a third source of energy, and the main focus for endurance training, is available.

Our most important long term energy source comes from the aerobic system. Its characteristic feature is that significant amounts of energy can be derived from the conversion of fat in the aerobic muscle fiber. The aerobic system, with its use of fat, has up to 75,000 kcal of energy available – enough abundant energy reserve to maintain training or racing for many hours, or even days.

Triglycerides are the main fats used for energy. When chemically broken down in fat stores they enter the bloodstream as free fatty acids (FFA), where they are carried to the aerobic muscles and burned in the mitochondria for energy. This process of burning fat is called beta oxidation.

In addition to burning fat, the aerobic system also uses some glucose for energy production. Even in the breakdown of triglycerides to FFA, glycerine which is normally stored in the fat molecule is released, converted to glucose and used for energy.

The utilization of glucose by the aerobic system is vital because it maintains the fat burning process. During training or racing, if you deplete your glucose and glycogen stores, fat burning will also cease.

Herein lies the endurance game; as the time of your activity increases, more fat and aerobic energy must be generated. But as the intensity increases, less oxygen is delivered so aerobic metabolism is diminished, forcing the body to use more anaerobic energy, which is much more limited. If you use up all your glucose, even fat burning stops, along with the rest of your body. Do you refrain from going faster so you can go farther? Can you really go father and faster?

You can have the best of both; the answer is in your training. By properly programming your body you can develop both endurance and aerobic speed, the focus of later chapters. It is also a program based on time and intensity, and is not miles and pace.

> *Another way of explaining this program is that you are able to burn a higher percentage of fat – and lower amounts of sugar – at higher levels of intensity.*

If you are not yet encouraged to focus more on aerobic instead of anaerobic training, here is another important factor. The percentage of aerobic and anaerobic activity in workouts or races of different duration is an important consideration. The list below indicates how much aerobic and anaerobic energy is used during maximal activity.

Time (minutes)	Percent Anaerobic	Percent Aerobic
1	70	30
2	50	50
4	35	65
10	15	85
30	5	95
60	2	98
120	1	99
>120	<1	>99

This is an extremely brief view of the body's metabolism. The chemical activity which takes place in the body every moment during training and racing, and at rest, is very complex. For example, there are at least 900 enzymes known to be involved with metabolism. Just the breakdown of sugar to energy requires 19 different chemical reactions. And it's not just the metabolism that is complex, but all the systems of the body.

One final note about our discussion on the different aspects of the body – neurological, muscular and metabolic – and their role in training. It has been my observation that each aspect of the body progresses at slightly different rates. You may perceive this in different ways.

Your perceived exertion at the same intensity may not always feel the same. For example, when athletes first start on my program, the biggest complaint is they don't feel they are getting much of a workout because of the relatively slow pace. During that phase, the muscles are more developed than the aerobic metabolism. But in time, this situation changes.

By developing your aerobic metabolism you are eventually able to train at a faster rate with less effort. You may then have more physical difficulty because your muscular and neurological body has not kept pace with the progressing aerobic metabolism. Athletes may complain that, despite a low training heart rate they have to work very hard.

Training is much like conducting a symphony; there are many players which must be working in precise harmony to produce a great performance. We have talked about three main parts of the body and their effect on and from training. But as you can see, each part has many smaller pieces that are vital to the success of the whole.

Chapter 5

The Original MAF Heart Rate Monitor Program

The information in this book provides you with the basic tools necessary to improve not only your endurance, but your health too. As endurance improves, you'll notice your speed increases, which makes for better competitive performance. Another benefit is that these gains continue for years and decades.

Continued development comes with objective, self-evaluation you make throughout the year. This is necessary so you can fine tune your training and avoid the potential dangers. Effective evaluation is accomplished by understanding some simple techniques and using a heart rate monitor as a biofeedback tool.

Dorland's Medical Dictionary defines biofeedback as "the process of providing visual or auditory evidence to a person of the status of body function so that you may exert control over that function."

As a student involved in a biofeedback research project, I measured responses in human subjects to various physiological inputs; sounds, visual effects, and various physical stimulation including activity. The observed reactions were evaluated by measuring temperature, sweating and heart rate.

It became evident that using the heart rate to objectively measure body function was simple, accurate and useful. And its application in sports was obvious.

There are three important applications for endurance athletes using a heart rate monitor:

- training
- assessment
- racing

Essentially, what is being measured is the maximum aerobic function – MAF – of the athlete. This can be done during swimming, biking, running or any endurance activity. The MAF is the foundation of endurance efficiency; it is where speed and stamina comes from, and how your performance improves through your years in the sport.

Before discussing the specifics of training, assessment and racing, I would like to give you a historical perspective of how this program was developed.

In my early years in practice in the late 70s, a large, bulky heart rate unit was on the market which I used on an increased number of athletes to monitor training. More specifically, it was a way to appraise the quality of the workout – was the athlete working too hard for the prescribed training, or perhaps not strenuous enough?

Previous to having a heart monitor available, the pulse rates were determined manually. At first, the athletes would take their own pulse. But I found their accuracy was generally not good; they usually arrived at heart rates too low compared to the actual rate determined by pulse meters. When I took the pulse of the athlete, the same problem occurred. But the difficulty getting an accurate number was not one of counting, but of the athletes recovery. Usually, the athlete would have to slow or stop to check the pulse, which would cause the heart rate to diminish quickly resulting in an inaccurate number.

There is another problem with manually taking your pulse. If you place your fingers on the carotid artery on the side of your neck, the pulse can easily be found. However, this area is also sensitive. Applying even moderate pressure here can severely effect the heart rate, blood flow to the brain and oxygen delivery. This is because the carotid area contains nerve ending which normally send messages to the brain indicating blood pressure changes. Stimulating this area with pressure sends an improper message to the brain, which slows the heart, sometimes quite dramatically. Not only will this lower your heart rate significantly, but it can be dangerous. The oxygen debt created can cause fainting (or death in an extreme case).

The advent of heart monitors which sensed the heart rate directly from the chest wall was a great benefit. I was finally able to get accurate readings without interrupting the workout.

Initially, athletes would use the monitor once per week, on the track or riding their bike. They would come to my clinic where we would strap the monitor on and they would go out for their workout. At the same time, I would observe their gait (their posture during the workout) and correlate their mechanical efficiency with the heart rate.

During these assessment sessions, I was able to give the athlete a better idea of how fast, or slow, they should be training. It soon became evident that the athletes needed more consistent training quality, rather than them relying on the feel of the workout on the day they used the heart monitor. It became necessary for each athlete to have their own heart monitor and train with it every day. Some bought their own monitors and used them during each workout.

One of the most significant observations I made was that athletes who wore their heart rate monitors during each workout felt better, and improved in performance at a faster rate than others who trained without a monitor.

Up until this time, the training heart rate we chose was based on how the athlete looked during our assessments of them on the track or road. Previous to that I knew that the number I found to be ideal in my assessment was different than the standard formula promoted traditionally, that of the 220 formula. This method stated that the age subtracted from 220, which is the maximum heart rate, multiplied by a certain percentage – from 65 to 85 percent – was a good training heart rate. Since everyone is unique, this general formula made little sense to me.

As my athletic practice became larger, it was necessary to find another method of determining which heart rate was best for a given athlete. More clues would come from laboratory information.

By measuring RQ – the amount of fat and sugar an athlete was burning – and correlating that with the heart rate, it became easier to obtain an ideal training heart rate for a given athlete.

These numbers were correlated with the ones determined from empirical data I made on the track or road, where the only assessment was the observation of gait. It was obvious to me that the most efficient mechanical movement of the athlete during an endurance workout correlated with a high percentage of fat burning. (Not the highest percentage of fat burning. This would be associated with the lowest levels of training.)

Training for endurance requires high amounts of fat burning, with more of it needed for increased endurance. In time, other vital observations were made: the relationship between training at the prescribed heart rate and the ability to burn more fat at the same heart rate. And, the relationship of these changes to a lowered RQ and an increased speed.

Even more important was the fact that by incorporating higher heart rate training too often, the same progress did not follow, i.e. increased fat burning would usually not occur. This combined well the theory promoted by New Zealand coach Arthur Lydiard, who said endurance athletes needed to build an aerobic base to improve performance.

Still missing was the ability for anyone to determine their maximum aerobic heart rate, as I now called it. Training at this heart rate would improve endurance and performance, burn more fat and improve the overall health of the athlete. This meant a new formula had to be created, one which took into account as many factors as possible including the individual athlete's uniqueness.

Chapter 6

The 180-Formula

The older methods of determining one's training level were typically the talk test, or the 220 formula. The 180-Formula replaces both.

You may be familiar with the talk test, which assumes you are exercising within the aerobic range if you can comfortably talk to your training partners during a workout. This test is not reliable and often maintains someone in an mild anaerobic state for weeks or months before the person realizes what is happening.

Another formula, unfortunately still widely used today, asks you to subtract your age from 220 and multiply the difference by a figure ranging from 65 to 85 percent. The resulting number supposedly provides you with your proper training heart rate.

This old formula contains two errors. It assumes that 220 minus your age is your maximum heart rate. In reality, most athletes who obtain their maximum heart rate by pushing themselves to exhaustion will find it is probably not 220 minus their age. About a third find their maximum is above, a third will be below and only a third may be close to 220 minus their age.

The second inaccuracy is the multiplier, which can be 65% to 85%. This arbitrary figure doesn't consider an athlete's overall health or fitness. Do you use 65% or 75%? How about 80% or 70%? Without having a more precise indicator, you are left to chance. And most athletes guess a number that offers a higher heart rate.

Rather than guess, it's best to use a formula which is not only more sensible, but more scientific: the 180-Formula. This method also considers physiological rather than just chronological age.

The 180-Formula: Finding Your Maximum Aerobic Heart Rate

1. Subtract your age from 180 (180 - age)

2. Modify this number by selecting one of the following categories:

   a. If you have, or are recovering from, a major illness (heart disease, any operation, any hospital stay, etc.) or if you are on any regular medication,
   ....subtract 10

   b. If you have not exercised before, or if you have been exercising but have been injured or are regressing in your training or competition, or if you often get colds or flu, or have allergies,
   .... subtract 5

   c. If you have been exercising for up to two years without any real problems, and if you have not had colds or flu more than once or twice per year,
   ....subtract 0

   d. If you have been exercising for more than two years without any problems, while making progress in competition, without injury,
   ....add 5

For example, if you are 30 years old and fit into Category b:
180 - 30 = 150, then 150 - 5 = 145 beats per minute.
This is your maximum aerobic heart rate.

In this example, exercising at a heart rate of 145 beats per minute will be highly aerobic, allowing you to properly and maximally develop endurance. Above that, there's a rapid change to more anaerobic function, exemplified by a shift to more sugar and less fat burning.

Initially, training at this relatively low rate may be stressful for many athletes. "I just can't train that slow!," is a common comment. But after a short time, you will feel better and your pace will quicken at that same heart rate. You will not be stuck training at that relatively slow pace for too long. Still, for many athletes it is difficult to change bad habits.

Case History

Don was a good athlete who usually placed in the top of his age group. When he came to my clinic with chronic injuries, fatigue and recurrent colds, one of the first things we did was test him on the track with a heart monitor. At his max aerobic heart rate Don was only able to run at an 8:40 pace – almost 2 minutes slower than his usual training pace! I recommended that Don train at this pace with a monitor for a three month base period. But two weeks later he called me and said it was impossible to run that slow. I again explained the whole process and how he would get faster. A week later he faxed me a letter and said he could not train by my recommendations. Several months later, Don came back to the clinic with more serious symptoms. Now he was ready to train aerobically. It took several more months for Don to increase his aerobic pace until finally he was running his "normal" 6:45 pace; but this time at a heart rate that was 25 beats less.

Most heart rate monitors can be set for different ranges, providing you with an audible indication if your heart rate goes over or under your pre-set levels. Set yours at the maximum aerobic rate you determined. In the example above, the monitor would be set for a maximum pulse of 145. Most monitors also provide for a low setting, which could be 10 below the high. This gives you a comfortable range to work out in. In this example, the low would be 135. Therefore, the range for an athlete with a maximum aerobic rate of 145 would be 135-145.

A frequently asked question by multisport athletes is, should different heart rates be used for different endurance sports? The answer is no, all aerobic training activity utilizes the 180-Formula.

At the same heart rate, different endurance sports require the same levels of metabolic activity. So whether you're swimming, biking or running, many physiologic parameters are the same.

But other aspects are quite different when comparing swimming, for example, to running. One significant difference is perceived exertion, which is a subjective feeling the athlete has in relation to the workout.

Another difference, a very objective one, is gravity stress. The difference in this stress between swimming and running is dramatic; there is very little gravity influence in the water, but that same force is maximally effecting the body during running. A lot of energy may not have to go into countering gravity stress in the pool but just the opposite is true during a run.

As a result, the heart rate during swimming is lower compared to running at the same effort, since the stress level is diminished in the water. Another way of looking at this phenomenon is to compare perceived exertion at the same heart rate. Swimming at a heart rate of 145 feels more difficult compared to running at the same heart rate, which feels relatively easy. (This is true if you are equally trained in both disciplines.)

In relation to the stress of swimming and running, cycling falls between the two, along with cross country skiing, skating and most other endurance activities. In these actions, there is some gravity stress along with mechanical stress.

Another factor that influences the heart rate is technique. For the beginning swimmer, the heart rate is usually much higher. As you become more proficient, the stress level lowers and the same intensity results in lower heart rates.

The benefits of training with a heart monitor are many, and only with time and experience will you come to truly appreciate them.

Another significant benefit of applying the 180-Formula to heart rate training is the chemical response by the body to training at that relatively lower level of intensity.

Normally, the body produces chemicals called oxygen free radicals in response to many stresses, including certain types of training. While these chemicals can be helpful, too many contribute to degenerative problems such as inflammatory condition, heart disease and cancer. In addition, increased free radicals speed the aging process.

High intensity, anaerobic training produces large amounts of free radicals. This is the reason some professionals suggest limiting your training. But even moderate training intensities can produce free radicals. However, using the 180-Formula as your guide, free radical production is minimized. Studies show that training at this efficient intensity is ideal when free radical stress is a concern.

Chapter 7

The MAF Test

One of the many benefits of this program is that you will generate more speed with the same effort. This is true not only of training speed but race pace as well. Another advantage of using a heart rate monitor is the ability to objectively measure these improvements using the Maximum Aerobic Function Test, or the MAF Test.

The MAF Test objectively measures the improvements you make in aerobic speed due to the progress made by the aerobic system during base building. Without objective measurements, you run the risk of fooling yourself into thinking all is well with training.

The MAF Test can be performed using any endurance activity. Your goal is to measure how fast you can run, bike, skate, etc. at your aerobic maximum heart rate. Or, how far you can go in a give time frame.

During the MAF Test, use your maximum aerobic heart rate found with the 180-Formula. While working out at that heart rate, determine some parameter such as pace (minutes per mile), speed (miles per hour) or repetitions (i.e. laps in a pool) over time. The test can also be done on stationary equipment measuring watts.

If you want to test your max aerobic function during running, for example, perform the test on a track by running at your max aerobic heart rate. Running from three to five miles provides more information, although a one mile test still has value. (The test is done following a warm up.)

Below is an actual example of a MAF Test performed by running on a track, calculating time in minutes per mile:

Mile 1	8:21
Mile 2	8:27
Mile 3	8:38
Mile 4	8:44
Mile 5	8:49

As indicated above, it is normal to obtain slightly slower times over 5 miles. The slower your first mile, the more the time will slow between the first and fifth mile. For example, if your first mile is 10:17 pace, your fifth mile may turn out to be 11:20. On the other hand, if your first mile is faster, the difference between mile one and five is less. For example, if your first mile is 5:50, your fifth mile may be 6:14.

During any one MAF Test, your times should always get slower; the first mile should always be the fastest, and the last the slowest. If that's not the case, it usually means you have not warmed up enough. An example of this is if your first mile is 7:46 and your second is 7:39.

In addition, the MAF Test should show faster times as the weeks pass compared to previous tests. But usually only during the aerobic base building part of your training. For example, over several months, we can see the endurance progress in this actual case:

	April	May	June	July
Mile 1	8:21	8:11	7:57	7:44
Mile 2	8:27	8:18	8:05	7:52
Mile 3	8:38	8:26	8:10	7:59
Mile 4	8:44	8:33	8:17	8:09
Mile 5	8:49	8:39	8:24	8:15

During anaerobic training, improvement in time usually slows or stops. The reasons are discussed in a later chapter.

Performing a MAF Test on a bike is similar. Except on your bike you have a couple of effective ways to record the test. The best and easiest method is to pick a bike course that takes about 30 to 45 minutes to complete. Following a warm up, ride at your max aerobic heart rate, and record exactly how long it takes to ride the test course. As you progress, your times should get lower. Riding your course today, for example, may take 36 minutes and 50 seconds. In three weeks it may take you 35:30 and in another three weeks 34:15. After three months of base work, the same course now takes you 33 minutes flat.

Another option is to ride on a flat course and see how fast a pace you can maintain while holding your heart rate at your max aerobic level. This works best in a velodrome or indoors on a trainer or rollers. As you progress, your miles-per-hour should increase. If you start at 18 miles per hour, for example, following a three month aerobic base you could be riding 24 mph at the same heart rate.

Perform the MAF Test regularly, throughout the year, and chart your results. I recommend doing the test every three weeks. More often than that may result in mental stress; aerobic speed will usually not improve significantly within one week. Focusing on the test this often can foster an obsession much like that seen in athletes who are addicted to weighing themselves on the scale daily or even more often.

Performing the test irregularly or not often enough defeats one of its purposes; knowing when your training is going off course. If something interferes with your progress – training itself, diet, stress, etc. – you don't want to wait until you're feeling bad or racing poorly to find that out.

> *One of the great benefits of the MAF Test is its ability to objectively inform you of a obstacle long before you feel it or see it as an injury or declining performance.*

As with any evaluation, an important element of the MAF Test is knowing what is normal and what is not. During endurance training, you could encounter three different phases: progression, plateau and regression.

As I have said repeatedly, if you successfully develop your aerobic system you will generate more aerobic speed. This is the progressive phase of the program, and it can and should continue for many years without regression. However, this period may have phases of normal plateaus.

Initially, your progress will be measured by large improvements – less minutes per mile, more miles per hour or whatever parameters you choose to use. As time goes on and development continues, progress occurs at a slower rate. The graph on page 52 represents actual progress of an age-group cyclist over a four year period. Notice the plateaus scattered throughout the period.

There are actually two different kinds of plateaus; one is normal and the other unhealthy.

With improvement, you will eventually arrive at a normal leveling off – almost as if your body needs a rest from the progress it's making. The reason for this is unclear, although it seems like the metabolic, neurological and muscular aspects of the body require a period of adjustment. It may also be related to the need for recovery, much like ascending a long hill. These normal plateaus should not last too long; a few weeks to a month

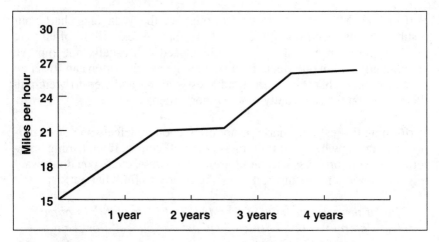

or two at most. At the end of that time, progress should again resume as measured by the MAF Test. But if you stay in your plateau for longer periods, it may be abnormal.

An abnormal plateau is due to some obstacle which prevents progress. The MAF Test is very useful to help diagnose an abnormal plateau. Once you find your times have stayed the same for too long, the next step is to find out why. Specifically, what is interfering with your progress. There could be many factors.

By far the most common reason for an abnormal plateau is stress. Recall that stress can be physical, chemical or mental. Typically, some lifestyle stress, often more than one, will cause your body to plateau. The weather may also be a stress which can halt endurance progression.

Case History
Karen's progress was rapid, almost from the moment she began the program. Her first mile MAF Test on the track went from 9:07 pace in September to 7:52 the following June But after that improvement there was a long three month plateau. Finally, progress was restored. The next year the same pattern was evident: great progress only to be halted abruptly by three months of no improvements. At first I thought Karen's plateaus were normal. Eventually, I considered the possibility that perhaps her tolerance to the summer weather – hazy, hot and humid conditions – was too much of a stress, and this was the cause of the plateau. Since

Karen could not go to the mountains for the summer to avoid the weather stress, we cut her training schedule down by about 30%. Using that strategy beginning in the late spring, Karen continued progressing through the next summer. She also felt better than normal, and continued racing better than the previous year.

If you think your plateau is abnormal, assess yourself carefully, or get help from a professional who understands the needs of endurance athletes. Find out what is blocking your natural progress. In addition to stress, other common deterrents include overtraining, dehydration, poor diet and nutritional problems.

Even worse than not making progress is regressing. Indeed, that is just what happens if your plateau is prolonged. An abnormal plateau resulting from some type of stress or factors mentioned above will eventually cause your MAF Test to get worse each time you check it. If this happens, your body is in a "red alert" and you should be very cautious. This is the time when you become most vulnerable to injury and ill health. In this case, one recommended strategy is to cut your training by 50%. This will assure more rest and recovery. Another suggestion is to stop all anaerobic workouts, including racing. For some athletes, both recommendations are worthy of serious consideration.

In addition, assess yourself as you did above; your training, racing, life stress, and so on. Find out why the natural progress which should be taking place is not only not happening, but your good intentions are making you worse.

During the early stages of regression you may not necessarily notice yourself with an injury or feeling bad. Those obvious signs and symptoms occur in the later stages of deteriorating endurance. There may not be any early symptoms. Even blood tests may appear normal. The only sign that something is wrong may come from your MAF Test.

If you do not respect the advice of your body, which during the MAF Test indicated you were regressing, you may ultimately be seeking first aid advice from a professional. This due to exhaustion, injury, sickness or some other major breakdown, possibly including one on a mental level. Lowered endurance parallels poor health; declining health corresponds to endurance regression.

A decline in endurance is so common, that many athletes and coaches think it's normal; it's not. This common notion has given birth to the myth of "the peak." This belief asserts that you build up your ability, progress to a high level where race performance is a its highest, then you fall off. When you decline from this peak, you perform poorly.

Rather than the philosophy of a peak, I promote one of continued improvement throughout the race year, with each race better than the next. But can we really analyze endurance races that closely? I don't think so. Each competition has with it so many variables; weather, travel factors, different terrain and so on. So rather than focusing on analyzing something as subjective as the race, focus on getting as healthy and fit as you can, and use the MAF Test to objectively measure progress.

The MAF Test can be applied to any endurance activity. While it is not a classic double blind scientific study, it still maintains the reproducibility important for objective, ongoing evaluations.

There are a number of factors which may effect your test results. When running, for example, the type of track surface may have a slight influence on your pace. The modern high tech track surfaces result in a fastest pace, whereas the old cinder tracks will slow your pace at the same heart rate. Uneven tracks will give slower times compared to perfectly flat surfaces. The ideal situation is to have an indoor track. But beware, too short a track will generally cause a slightly slower pace due to the increased turning.

On your bike, a velodrome is ideal but not accessible for most athletes. The roughness or smoothness of the road surface, its varying grades and traffic will all effect your test results. The net result of hills usually is a worsening of pace, unless there are significantly more downhills. A good option is to use a wind trainer or rollers.

Usually, these factors, and the others described below, can make a difference of five to eight seconds per mile on a track or two to three miles per hour on your bike, possibly more. But to assure the MAF Test is most accurate, be consistent; use the same course or method each time you perform the test. In the event that you change your test course, be sure to note it in your diary or chart.

Other factors which potentially interfere with your test include the weather, altitude, hydration and your equipment. Most of these factors can work against you by increasing your physical effort, which increases the heart rate. Since you are working at a specific heart rate, the result is a slower pace. Again, the minimal amount of influence should not pose a real problem. Rather, you should just be aware of these factors.

The weather influences your body, and therefore the MAF Test, in several ways:

• A head wind may physically counter your forward motion, raising your heart rate. A tail wind will have the opposite effect; you'll go faster at the same heart rate.

• Temperature may also be a factor during your test. Extremes of heat and cold will raise your heart rate forcing you to slow down.

• High humidity can act much like a head wind. It is a physical barrier of water which you must work through. The increased effort raises your heart rate and results in a slower test.

• Rain and snow are similar to humidity and head winds. Going through rain (and to a lesser extent snow) requires more effort. In addition, if the surface you are on is wet with water and especially snow, additional physical effort is required.

• Barometric pressure can also have a slowing effect on your MAF Test. Low barometric pressure results in a slightly lower oxygen uptake. The result is less oxygen gets to your muscles and your body compensates by raising the heart rate.

Often, weather stress is not the result of a single factor. A combination of cold and wind, for example, can elevate the heart rate significantly. Summer heat, humidity and low pressure, sometimes referred to as the "dog days of August," can also stress your body and raise the heart rate.

For these reasons, if you arrive at your MAF Test day and the weather is extreme, wait a day or more until the weather stress has lessened.

Altitude can have a significant effect on the body and MAF Test, especially if you have not had a chance to adapt to a new altitude. If you're headed for the mountains to train for a period of time, wait a week or more until you adjust to the altitude before performing your MAF Test. Even then, your times generally slow when you ascend to higher altitudes, and when descending to lower altitudes, you MAF Test improves.

Hydration also effects your aerobic pace. Even slight dehydration can slow you down. Once you dehydrate, it may take 24 hours or longer to rehydrate, no matter how much water you consume. It's important to drink smaller amounts of water all day rather than large amounts a couple of times a day.

Your equipment can also effect the outcome of your MAF Test. The two most significant items are your bike and running shoes.

Your bike set up and positioning, the pressure and wear on your tires and any other factors that change drag, such as clothing, will slow your MAF Test. Make a note in your diary if your test is done with a different bike set up, more clothing or other factors that may change the test.

Running shoes will also effect the results of your MAF Test. In general, shoes with more cushioning and more support, and heavier shoes all slow you down. Lighter shoes, including racing styles, generally allow you to run faster at the same heart rate.

While most of the above factors will raise your heart rate and slow your pace or speed, performing the MAF Test for longer rather than shorter times will help compensate for these natural errors. For running, this means 5 miles, for a bike test, a total of about 30 to 45 minutes or more.

One other factor that will effect your MAF Test is worth mentioning here. Ill health. When you are sick, your body's immune system is working very hard to recover, and it needs all the energy it can get. The last thing your body wants to do is work out. Especially when you have an elevated temperature. In this situation, don't train or race. If you've ever attempted this, and worn a heart monitor, you know what happens; your heart rate elevates, sometimes drastically. The same effect is observed if you are anemic; less oxygen can be delivered to the muscles, with the resulting MAF Test being slower.

Some Factors Which Effect the MAF Test

Factor	Effect on MAF Test
Running tracks:	
All-weather	improves
Dirt, grass, cinder	worsens
Indoor	improves
400-meter	improves
200-meter	worsens
Bike or skate:	
Velodrome	improves
Smooth road	improves
Rough road	worsens
Hills	worsens
Weather:	
Wind	worsens
Rain/snow	worsens
Humidity	worsens
Low barometric pressure	worsens
Very high/low temperature	worsens
Altitude	
Higher	worsens
Lower	improves

Another important aspect of the MAF Test is that it is indicative of performance. A direct relationship exists between your aerobic pace and race effort. In other words, as your MAF Test improves, so will your racing ability, *even if you have not done speed work.*

In the early 1980s, I collected a lot of MAF data on runners. Back then, it was called maximum aerobic pace (MAP), but as all other types of athletes began to use the test, "pace" was changed to "function." In addition, the data runners could provide was more objective because we could control more variables.

After hundreds of tests and several racing seasons, it was evident that the pace a runner could perform at their aerobic maximum pace was positively correlated with their race pace. The race distances varied, but more data was gathered for 5K and 10K distances. The chart below, based on actual data, is an example of the relationship between MAF and 5K race performance.

MAF and Performance

MAF (min per mile)	5K Race Pace	5K Time
10:00	7:30	23:18
9:00	7:00	21:45
8:30	6:45	20:58
8:00	6:30	20:12
7:30	6:00	18:38
7:00	5:30	17:05
6:30	5:15	16:19
6:00	5:00	15:32
5:45	4:45	14:45
5:30	4:30	13:59
5:15	4:20	13:28
5:00	4:15	13:12

Through the years it also became obvious that all endurance events – triathlons, marathons, cycling events, swimming – could be improved by developing a faster aerobic pace.

A note for multisport athletes: If you are training for more than one or two events, you may frequently be at a plateau for one event. For example, if you are measuring progress in swimming, biking and running, you may see your swim and run times improving while your bike has plateaued. After a couple of months, this may change with swimming and cycling showing progress while your running maintains an even level. The reason for this is unclear, but I feel it is a normal part of progression.

The Big Picture
Are you confused with all the terminology? Don't worry, just follow the basic rules and your training will progress. Don't get caught up in the definitions; they don't all fit neatly together. That's not only true with mine, but sometimes within the field of exercise physiology.

Two phrases that should be differentiated are maximum aerobic function and anaerobic threshold. They are obviously different states.

The maximum aerobic function is an endurance state where fat burning is a significant part of the energy requirement. Often, in a properly trained athlete, fat is the primary fuel during MAF levels, sometimes accounting for up to 75% of the energy needs. As a result, there is less dependency on glucose for energy needs, and minimal lactic acid is produced. Generally, the percentage of maximum heart rate which corresponds the maximum aerobic level is relatively low; usually about 70%, although this often varies with each athlete.

The definition of anaerobic threshold is the point at which the body's metabolism can no longer meet its energy demand predominantly by aerobic function. As a result, anaerobic metabolism increases significantly, along with lactic acid. Glucose becomes the primary fuel and fat burning is greatly diminished. The percentage of maximum heart rate that corresponds to anaerobic threshold varies greatly, depending on training; it can be as high as 80% but can also be below 70%.

The chart below incorporates these concepts, along with some others including respiratory quotient.

Training Levels	% Max HR*	Substrate Utilization† (% Carbo and Fat)	
Max HR	100	Max	Higher
Max Anaerobic Training	90		
Anaerobic Threshold (Lactate Threshold)			
		Glucose — Fat — RQ	
Aerobic Maximum			
			Lower
		Max	
Recovery	Rest		

(Anaerobic ↑ / Aerobic ↓)

* Related heart rates vary with each athlete.
† Percentage of carbohydrate and fat varies with each athlete and changes with training.

Chapter 8

The Overtraining Syndrome

Overtraining is an imbalance of the training equation: too much working out, too little rest or both. The problem has reached epidemic proportions within the athletic community. Through my years in practice, two-thirds of the athletes initially seen were overtrained.

I want to discuss some of the many aspects of overtraining, referred to as the Overtraining Syndrome, before going on to the specifics of efficient training.

The three factors I emphasize for improved endurance are the same ones that prevent overtraining:

- The importance of aerobic training.
- The diminished need for anaerobic training.
- The fact that overtraining is usually preceded by too much anaerobic work or racing.

The end results of overtraining are all too well known: physical and mental fatigue, poor performance, and injury. But the best clue that we're over doing it occurs long before discomfort and ill health. That indication is often that you not only feel great, but experience sometimes outstanding performances and sense your body is infallible. Many athletes refer to this period as their "peak." Rather than hitting a peak, which is often followed by a drop in performance, a long build-up of constant improvement year after year is best. This will help prevent the overtraining syndrome from developing.

Training involves slightly overloading the body, then allowing it to rest and recover. Too much overload or too little rest and recovery eventually produces overtraining. The time needed to produce an overtrained athlete varies with each person, how much work is done, and how much rest is obtained.

Overtraining results in a state of physical, chemical and mental imbalance; a consequence of training beyond the body's ability to compensate for the workloads placed upon it. The neurological, metabolic, muscular aspects of the body simply become overextended to the point where they can no longer work in harmony with each other. In other words, you burn out.

Case History

> *Jill was not unlike many case histories in this book; she tried to fit all her training on top of an otherwise very busy week. As the months went by, her diary showed a clear indication that overtraining was inevitable. Over a six month period, her morning heart rate slowly increased, her MAF did not improve and her racing deteriorated. Even worse was the fact that Jill continued her routine. It was not until, as she said, "everything completely crashed" that she thought anything was wrong.*

The Overtraining Syndrome is relatively simple to diagnose, although the problem is easily and often overlooked. Recognizing it requires making a good objective assessment of yourself, including a review of your training and racing schedule and performance, your mental and physical state, and sometimes other factors which can be measured by a professional such as blood pressure and laboratory tests. Unfortunately, if you regress to the point where overtraining is observed in the blood pressure or blood, you're well entrenched into the problem.

The relative ease of assessing the overtraining syndrome also illustrates the fact that it is easily preventable. But most of the time, the athlete runs too far into overtraining before realizing it's time to do something. An important component of training is the ability to objectively measure your training direction and modify it before damage is done.

The process of overtraining is something difficult to define. It's not a number in a lab report, or a measurement of normals and abnormals. Recognizing it in the earliest possible stages is necessary, and should almost be a daily self-assessment.

The physical aspects are easiest to see. The muscles are either not given enough time to recover or are simply pushed beyond their abilities too often. Either situation results in dysfunction of specific muscles, and their inability to work in unison with other muscles. The end result may be pain or loss of proper mechanical function. Since muscles control bones and joints, these areas may also become symptomatic; pain, swelling and dysfunction are clear indications something is wrong.

The chemical aspect of over stimulating the neurological and metabolic aspects of the body, which among other things contributes indirectly to physical injuries, is a major part of the Overtraining Syndrome. Like any bad habit, your nerves "learn" overtraining, resulting in more difficulty in changing training habits.

During overtraining, an important part of body chemistry – the adrenal glands – simply becomes exhausted. As a result, even recovery from an easy workout is impaired.

Can we look at just one point in your training cycle and predict you're headed for overtraining? Not always. There are some good, successful training schedules that, if maintained too long would end in overtraining. To make our meaning more complete, defining overtraining should include a time relationship. Maintaining a certain part of your program for too long, such as too many long rides, or too much anaerobic intervals, may contribute to the overtraining syndrome.

Certainly training must include intensities high enough to stress the body so it can continue to build itself up and withstand the burden of racing. But there's a limit. And if we continue at too high a level of intensity for too long, without the proper schedule change, we become overtrained.

So, in addition to time, another component of overtraining is change – the need to alter your program at the right intervals. This need arises because of your body's requirements change, and you must keep up with them. So if you maintain a specific regiment – even a very successful one – it eventually may need to be changed.

How long can you continue the same weekly schedule before you risk overtraining? That, of course, depends on the person – everyone is different. It may take from a few months to a year or two to burn out if you keep on a schedule not tailored to your needs. For the beginner, it may take longer. During this time – a period we'll call pre-overtraining, or pre-OT – some interesting events occur.

During pre-OT, you may still increase your oxygen uptake, get stronger and faster, and even burn more fat. You may lose weight, and even start to feel good. So good you're sure you're on the right track. As you progress into your pre-OT period, you start performing well; Sometimes so well that others start following your program. You even have a few great races and maybe, with a little luck, the season of your dreams.

But then, as the overtraining syndrome evolves, you wake up from the dream. Your pre-OT period deteriorates to you simply being overtrained. You may have a bad race, then another and another. By now you're more tired than you used to be. And if all this is accompanied by a physical injury, you're wondering where the fun has gone, or if your athletic life is over. Or worse, you ask yourself if you're too old to be doing this.

If you have to ask yourself if you're overtrained, it may be the first clue that you are. How do you know when to stop and modify your schedule? More importantly, how do you assess yourself?

By far the best way to evaluate yourself and prevent from overtraining is by the MAF Test. Every three weeks, record your test results and keep a constant eye out for changes. An abnormal plateau or a regression phase as discussed previously is synonymous with overtraining.

In addition, consider these other important assessment tips:

1. Keep tabs on your morning heart rate. It should not increase over long periods of time. But beware; in some people overtraining is accompanied by a lowering of the heart rate.

2. Keep a diary. Just the act of writing down what you do – including how you feel, everything and anything about your training, racing and life – is a good way to assess yourself.

3. Get someone with an objective eye to assist you in your training or at least in evaluating your schedule. Or, if you know someone you have confidence in, use them as a coach.

4. Learn to read your body. The pre-OT zone is full of subtle clues that you're not going in the right direction. Little physical twinges, inexplicable but almost unnoticed symptoms of sleep irregularity, changes in appetite – especially cravings for sugar or caffeine – are important clues. Make notes about any of these hints in your diary, and look for a pattern of repetition.

5. Get input from your spouse or significant other.

Clearly, the best way to handle overtraining is to avoid it. Prevention is the ideal approach. And honesty is your best policy.

Chapter 9

Warming Up and Cooling Down

When the topic of warming up is mentioned, for most people, stretching comes to mind first. While stretching is an important feature in sprint sports, it is much less significant, and too often harmful, in training for endurance.

Warming up refers to preparation of the body for training. The warming occurs partly from an increase in circulation of blood.

With the onset of your workout, the muscles quickly require much more oxygen and other nutrients, and have waste products that must be removed. This request by the muscles is accomplished by an increase in blood circulation. As discussed earlier, the aerobic muscle are well endowed with blood vessels, and most of the circulation is directed there.

Another aspect of warming up, one dependant upon increased circulation, is the increase in fats. As the muscles receive their increased blood flow, fats, in a form referred to as free fatty acids, also make themselves available for use as an energy source by the aerobic muscles.

If the muscles are receiving more blood, where does it come from? The answer to this question is the most important and significant aspect of warming up.

At rest, your body devotes much of its circulation to the organs and glands – the liver, adrenals, brain and spinal cord, etc. From a standpoint of blood circulation, this resting state is just the opposite of working out.

When you begin your workout, and the muscles obtain more circulation, more than half of the blood flow going to the organs and glands gets detoured into the working muscles. During an anaerobic workout, up to 80% of the blood is shifted to the muscles. While this satisfies the muscle's demands, the organs and glands all of a sudden may lack the circulation necessary for optimal function. In many ways, this is a major stress to the organs and glands when the shift occurs too quickly.

The remedy – the way to satisfy the whole body – has to do with timing. If the organs and glands slowly relinquish its circulation, at the same time the blood flow to the muscles is gradually increased, the potential stress is minimized.

When this happens, the neurological, metabolic and muscular body is optimally prepared for the remaining part of the workout.

In order to accomplish this, the muscle action should begin very easy and gradually build up. Often, athletes start off their workout with too much intensity, which quickly shifts the blood flow from organs and glands potentially causing stress.

A heart monitor is a very helpful tool for warming up. Let's say you want to go for an aerobic workout, and your max aerobic heart rate is 140 (with a range of 130-140). As you step out the door you notice your heart rate is 60. A proper warm up would dictate that you reach your 140 heart rate only after about 15 minutes for most workouts. Slowly raise your heart rate from the 60s to the 70s, 80s, etc. until you reach the 130-140 range after 15 minutes. For training lasting more than about 90 minutes, the warm up should be extended – perhaps to about 20 minutes or more.

Ideally, your warm up should be tailored to your body's needs. Once you get used to warming up properly, you may notice your body requiring more warm up time, even for a short workout. If this is the case, heed your body's signal and extend your warm up time. Never assume, however, that you need less than 15 minutes of warm up.

Cooling Down
Once you have turned on your body and provided it with a workout, the final stage is recovery. This is initiated with a cool down.

The cool down is just the opposite of a warm up; slowly allow the heart rate to descend. While you will not reach your starting heart rate, you may come within 10 or 20 beats of it. For example, if you headed out the door at a heart rate of 60, a proper cool down may bring you back to 70-80.

This slow decent in intensity prevents physical and chemical stress, especially within the cardiovascular system and the muscle fibers.

For most workouts, spend about 15 minutes cooling down. For longer workouts, such as 4 or more hours, increase this time to at least 20-30 minutes.

The main benefit of the cool down is it begins the process of recovery from the workout by assuring more blood flow is returned to the organs and glands.

The graph below plots heart rate and time, and indicates the proper warm up and cool down.

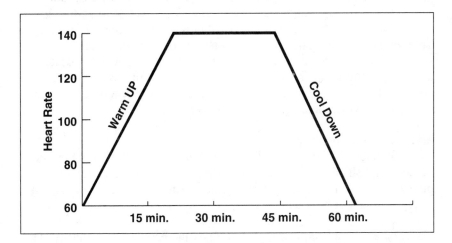

The graph below illustrates the incorrect way to warm up and cool down. In this case, the heart rate jumps immediately to the training level. At the end of the workout, the heart rate descends too quickly.

The time spent warming up and cooling down is part of your total work-out – a very important portion. So, if you plan on a one hour aerobic run, you will spend 15 minutes warming up, 15 cooling down, and a half hour at your max aerobic level.

Let me repeat what was noted above: the warm up prepares your body for the workout, and the cool down initiates the recovery process. Don't be fooled into thinking that, because you don't feel like you're getting much of a workout that the warm up and cool down doesn't count as part of it. Tremendous health benefits are obtained through these aspects of your program. An overtrained athlete often has arrived in that state because of a lack of warming up and cooling down. Nagging injuries sometimes dis-appear when a long enough warm up precedes the workout. Even racing is improved when the body is properly warmed.

Stretching vs. Flexibility

Many athletes associate stretching with warming up. But stretching does not accomplish what a real warm up does. Many also think stretching will prevent injury and improve performance. Not only is this not true, but often, just the opposite can occur.

It's very important, however, that athletes increase their flexibility. This can be done with a proper warm up. Even patients with arthritis can improve flexibility with an aerobic warm up, as much as by stretching.

There are two basic types of stretching, referred to as static and ballistic. Static stretching is a very slow, deliberate movement, where you lightly stretch a muscle and hold it statically (unchanged) for 10-30 seconds. When properly done, this activity promotes relaxation of the muscle being stretched. Optimal static stretching requires that each muscle group be sequentially repeated three to four times. It also demands that the activity be done slow and not rushed.

There are two types of static stretching. Of these, active is much more safe than passive. Active stretching is accomplished by contracting the antago-nist muscle (the one opposite the muscle you're stretching). For example, to actively stretch the hamstring muscles, the quadriceps are contracted.

Passive stretching uses gravity or force by another body part or person to move a body segment to the end of its range of motion or beyond – the reason this form of stretching can so easily cause injury.

The second basic type of stretching is called ballistic. This is a "bouncing" method and is the most common type of stretching done by athletes and beginners. It makes use of the body's momentum to repeatedly stretch a joint position to or beyond the extremes of range of motion. Because this method is more rapid than static stretching, it activates the stretch reflex which increases tension in the muscle, rather than relaxation. This can result in micro-tearing of muscle fibers with resultant injury.

Ballistic stretching is the type most say they don't do, but most really employ. That's because most athletes are in a hurry when stretching before or after training. Pre-race tension tends to make one stretch in a more stressful and quick mode, forcing you to be more a ballistic stretcher.

Flexibility refers to the relative range of motion allowed at a joint. This is related to the tension in the muscles that move or restrict the joint.

The risk of injury is increased when;
- a joint flexibility is increased too much,
- a joint flexibility is greatly diminished,
- an imbalance in joint flexibility exists between left and right (or front and back) sides of the body.

A study of US Army recruits found that the least flexible and the most flexible were more than twice as likely to get injured compared to those whose joints had moderate flexibility.

Endurance athletes who do stretch generally are more injured than those who don't stretch. That has not only been my observation over nearly 20 years of treating athletes, but the opinion and observation of many other professionals. In addition, scientific studies support these observations.

One common example used to show the increased injury rate in stretchers versus non-stretchers is the hamstring muscles. It is both the most frequently injured muscle group, and the most stretched.

Halbertsma, in a study of men and women 20-38 years of age with tight/stiff hamstrings, states that "stretching exercises do not make short hamstrings any longer or less stiff."

Richard Dominguez, M.D., an orthopedic surgeon at Loyola University Medical Center and author of *Total Body Training* (Charles Scribner's

Sons, 1982) and *The Complete Book of Sports Medicine* (Encore Editions, 1979) also disapproves of stretching. "Flexibility should not be a goal in itself, but the result of... training. Strengthening the muscles around a joint naturally increases flexibility. If you can bend a joint beyond your ability to control it with muscle strength, you risk either tearing the muscles, tendons or ligaments that support the joint, or damaging the joint through abnormal pressure on it."

Among the specific stretches Dominguez says are most damaging are the yoga plow, hurdler's stretch, toe touching, and the stiff leg raise.

The types of injury created by stretching may be in the muscle itself, the tendon and ligament associated with that muscle, or even the joint controlled by that muscle.

Exercise repetition from swimming, biking running and other endurance sports results in an already slight overstretched state. The chemical reaction to stretching, whether from a normal workout or the act of stretching, increases the production of chemicals called prostaglandins, which increases inflammation. Adding more stretching only increases the potential for more inflammation.

Many athletes stretch thinking it will help performance. But studies show this is not the case. Static stretching not only does not improve athletic performance, but may actually hinder it.

For those who require a wider range of motion, stretching may be necessary. But these athletes include dancers, sprinters and gymnasts, and not endurance athletes.

Case History
Randy began his morning with 10 minutes of stretching. Then the first 15 minutes of his workout was spent climbing hills from his house in the valley. When he first used a heart monitor, his rate surged to 180 within five minutes. But he could not imagine how any of that was related to his low back pain. By performing manual muscle testing, we discovered that Randy's hamstring muscles were overstretched and weak, not helping to support his low back. Therefore the first recommendation was to stop stretching his already overstretched hamstrings. Within a couple of weeks the low back improved. This was followed by the difficult task of

adjusting the morning ride to avoid the hills. The only solution was for Randy to ride on his rollers for about 15 minutes before going out the door, then riding very slow until getting past the hills. When he was able to accomplish this, his chronic asthma also disappeared.

Yoga and other "whole body" flexibility activities are very different from stretching as I've described it above. When properly done, which involves a very slow, deliberate and easy motion, whole body flexibility activities are healthy, safe and very effective. Applied kinesiologist Sam Yanuck describes this well; "In all my years of martial training, I've learned to "stretch" like animals. They gently stretch the whole body at once, in a mild way, from the tip of the toes to the top of the head and to the ends of the fingers."

Chapter 10

Aerobic Training

By far, the most important aspect of training for endurance is developing the entire aerobic system. This includes good circulation, slow twitch muscle fiber development and the ability to burn large amounts of fat for energy. Diminishing performance, injury and ill health almost always stems from a lack of aerobic function.

In this chapter, I want to discuss several important aspects of aerobic training. These include building an aerobic base, aerobic intervals, downhill or neurological workouts, aerobic speed and walking.

The first step in producing a highly efficient aerobic system is building a large, solid aerobic base. This phase of your training is a period of time when all your workouts are aerobic. Specifically this means at or below your max aerobic heart rate determined by the 180-Formula. It means every workout is aerobic. That includes the Sunday group ride, Saturday's hilly run in the park and any other workouts where you're heavily influenced by other athletes or the terrain.

In addition, an aerobic base period also is void of weight lifting, since this is also an anaerobic workout. This is the part of training where discipline, dedication and hard work are important. Most athletes think these three mental attributes are related to toughing it out, grunting and training in pain. But it's sometimes harder than that: training properly during the aerobic phase, for many athletes, is the most difficult part of the program. It's the ability to go slow, despite what other athletes are doing, and saying.

Many athletes complain initially about the slowness of the pace. They say it's too easy. This relatively slow pace is normal, especially if you have not built a good aerobic base. If you don't feel like you've done much after an aerobic workout, you're on target.

For other athletes, those who have successfully built a good aerobic base, the aerobic pace is not always excessively easy. But you don't progress to that level overnight, and success means starting at the right point. For many, this means starting slow.

Although your aerobic training will feel too easy and you'll wonder if you're benefiting, your pace will quicken in time. This may happen in a matter of weeks depending on many factors; the main one being stress. For many, some stress is in the form of anaerobic work, for others it's work stress, and still for some a combination of stress. Sometimes it's just "life's stress."

It's easy to measure your progress, and very important that you do. The MAF Test can guide you through your base. If you're really building properly, you'll see your pace improve. But if you're knowingly or unknowingly sneaking in some anaerobic work, you risk slowing or stopping the base building process.

How does anaerobic work interfere with building an aerobic base? Before explaining that, here's the bottom line: Anaerobic work can dramatically interfere with aerobic and endurance development. The MAF Test, for example, shows a quicker plateau often followed by regression. In some athletes, it only takes one anaerobic workout or race per week during the aerobic base period to inhibit aerobic development. In others, daily stress levels, which chemically mimic anaerobic activity, are enough to inhibit aerobic progress. And often, nutritional and dietary problems limit base building.

There may be several reasons why anaerobic workouts can inhibit aerobic base building.

- Anaerobic training can decrease the number of aerobic muscle fibers, sometimes significantly. This can happen in just a few short weeks of improper training.

- The lactic acid produced during anaerobic training may inhibit the aerobic muscle enzymes which are necessary for aerobic metabolism.

- Anaerobic training raises your respiratory quotient. This means your percentage of energy derived from sugar increases and fat burning decreases. In time, this may force more anaerobic metabolism and less aerobic function.

- Stress also has a physiologic response in the body, and can inhibit the aerobic system. Stress is nearly synonymous with anaerobic training. Excess stress raises cortisol levels, which ultimately increases insulin levels, inhibiting fat burning and increasing sugar usage. This promotes anaerobic metabolism and inhibits aerobic activity.

• Nutrition and diet can also prevent you from building a good aerobic base. Too much dietary carbohydrate, including sweets, or too little essential fat from the diet can inhibit the aerobic system. In both instances, fat burning is inhibited.

When all the endurance ingredients are mixed properly, the aerobic base develops and your pace increases as shown by your MAF Test. As your workout pace increases, you develop more aerobic speed.

Aerobic speed means you're able to swim, bike, run, skate or ski at a faster pace with the same effort. You've successfully developed your metabolism so you convert more fat to energy. In addition to possessing more aerobic speed, your adrenal function can improve enabling you to handle stress better, you store less fat, stabilize blood sugar better and become less vulnerable to injury.

As your aerobic speed increases, so does your performance. That's because you're able to race at a faster pace with the same effort as measured by heart rate. In a real sense, increased aerobic speed equates to faster anaerobic speed.

While building your aerobic base, there is a technique which can develop more speed without becoming anaerobic. It's called a downhill or neurological workout. This activity, as the name implies, involves going downhill to relieve some of the gravity stress. This allows the heart rate to also go down. In order to maintain your aerobic maximum heart rate, you have to increase your effort, and this results in running, biking, skating, etc. at a much faster rate.

For example, at a heart rate of 145, if you can run at a 7:45 pace, then running down a hill at the same heart rate will force you to run much faster; perhaps a 6:50 pace.

Using a long downhill that's not too steep, you can train your nervous system to turn the legs over much quicker than would ordinarily occur during a run on a flat course. If you have a long steady downhill that takes you 10 or 15 minutes, or longer, to complete, you can derive great benefits, including quicker turn over with your legs, without the stress of an anaerobic workout.

Be sure the downhill is not too steep a grade, which may force you to overstride. Even on the right grade, your stride length should be about the same as if you were on level ground. If the downhill run takes 5 or 10 minutes, you can do "downhill repeats," slowly going back up the hill to start your course again. If you're lucky enough to find an easy downhill that takes you a longer time, that's great.

I often suggest one or two downhill workouts per week, not on consecutive days, during the base period. This workout can last 45 minutes to an hour and a half, including warm up and cool down. Because it's all aerobic, when you're done it will feel much like any other aerobic workout despite the quick pace. These workouts will also help you develop more aerobic speed because of their effect on the nervous system.

Once you have achieved a high level of aerobic speed, it may be difficult or impossible for you to reach your aerobic maximum heart rate, depending on the event. This is most true in the water, and cycling, skating or skiing on flat terrain.

At this stage of your development, you may be ready to add aerobic intervals to your program.

Aerobic intervals enable you to train at your aerobic maximum heart rate for short periods despite the difficulty in maintaining that level of activity. This is usually reserved for the lower gravity events like swimming, but cyclists, skaters and skiers often improve to that point.

You'll know when you're ready for aerobic intervals; riding or swimming at your max aerobic heart rate will be physically very difficult because the pace is too fast. It is just the opposite of what you feel when first starting this program, where the pace may be too slow.

Since you won't be able to maintain your max aerobic heart rate for the whole workout, you can perform a short interval at that level, then slow down for a period of time, then go back to the max aerobic level.

The chart below is an actual example of a cyclist's aerobic interval workout. His max aerobic heart rate is 150, and the total workout time is 90 minutes.

A 20 minute warm up.

A 10-minute segment consisting of 5 minutes at 150 heart rate, and 5 minutes at 125 heart rate.

This 10 minute segment is repeated 5 times (totaling 50 minutes).

A 20 minute cool down.

With all the different aspects of aerobic base building mentioned in this chapter – aerobic speed, downhill workouts and aerobic intervals – I have emphasized the importance of raising the heart rate to your maximum aerobic level. But what if you don't feel like working out with that high a heart rate on a given day? Will you still derive aerobic benefits?

The answer is yes, you will still receive aerobic benefits even if your heart rate is not at your maximum aerobic level. You actually burn a higher percentage of fat during this type of workout, and incorporate aerobic muscle fibers you may otherwise no use.

I have observed many athletes who initially did not wish to be competitive, but derived great aerobic benefits by training at lower aerobic levels – below their aerobic range. Adding more intense aerobic work onto that type of base often produces a great endurance athlete. Because of this, I often encourage competitors at certain times of the year to have "easy" days where the heart rate never reaches their max aerobic level.

Often, especially during the racing season, training every other day at these easy levels helps speed recovery, and at the same time builds the small aerobic muscle fibers important for aerobic function. This can have a very positive effect on racing because these muscle fibers help break down lactic acid, improve circulation and burn fat for energy.

In addition, this technique is most helpful preceding a long race like the Ironman or a stage race lasting several days. During the tapering process, which I recommend beginning about two weeks before the race, train at least every other day below your max aerobic level.

Training this way at key points during the season can also help maintain your high aerobic and anaerobic levels previously developed, while training less.

An even better approach to building the small aerobic muscles is to walk regularly as a workout. Whether you're a cyclist, swimmer, runner or skater, a once or twice a week walk can be very helpful – for the rookie competitor to the greatest endurance athlete. Spend at least an hour on your walk, more if you wish. In the beginning, an hour will seem like a long time. Eventually, an hour will seem too short and you may want to spend more time. You won't have too much success finding a training partner, but you may be better going it alone.

The walking workout can be done anytime in your schedule. It works especially well the day before a race.

Walking is not only physiologically beneficial, but also can help mentally. Use it as a meditation, to help you focus on your body and it's health.

Whatever your particular style of training schedule, the most important aspect is your aerobic base. Within that base, and the way to fine tune it, are specific techniques that increase your aerobic speed; they include downhill workouts, aerobic intervals and walking. In addition, performing the MAF Test helps qualify your overall training. With so much variation, building an aerobic base should be an interesting and exciting adventure.

Case History
John was in his fourth year of building a winter base, and his MAF was 7:10, down from 9:45 when he first began. His schedule looks like this:

Mon 6am – Easy 45 minute swim; 5:30pm – Easy 45 minute run.
Tues 6am – One hour swim at max aerobic heart rate; 5pm – Two hour bike: aerobic intervals.
Wed 6am – 90 minute run at max aerobic heart rate.
Thurs 6am – One hour swim at max aerobic heart rate.
Fri 6am – One hour downhill run.
Sat 8am – Three hour bike; 4:30pm – Easy 45 minute swim.
Sun 8am – Two hour bike (aerobic intervals) followed by a one hour run.

John also enters one or two races (usually 10K) during the winter months, often running a personal best.

Chapter 11

Anaerobic training

Once you have built sufficient aerobic function, your body may be ready to add anaerobic work. I say "may" because many endurance athletes can often bypass this part of training and rely instead on racing to get all the anaerobic stimulation necessary.

An important question to answer about anaerobic workouts is, when should you begin them? One answer I frequently give is, if in doubt about when to start, wait. Build more base.

The main purpose of anaerobic training is to build the fast twitch muscle fibers, thereby increasing anaerobic speed. For endurance athletes, maximum benefits can be achieved easily, and in as short a time as three to four weeks.

Anaerobic workouts can be treacherous domain. This risky training is frequently the cause of injuries, fatigued and poor performance.

Still, some athletes are able to benefit from anaerobic work if properly done. If this is your situation, I have two recommendations:

- keep it simple
- keep it short

Keep It Simple

By keeping it simple, I am referring to the specific types of workouts in each sport. Some anaerobic interval workouts have become so complicated that one requires a computer and an engineering degree to follow them.

After many years of assigning hundreds of styles of anaerobic intervals in many sports, I have concluded without a doubt that all of these different methods result in the same benefits when it comes to endurance athletes. Whether a runner does quarters or hill repeats, step-ups or fartlek, the anaerobic stimulation they receive will provide very similar if not identical results for their race. If the swimmer does varying distance intervals with any number of specific patterns offered by the many successful coaches in the sport, they will all obtain the same or identical benefits for endurance races.

83

The most significant concern with anaerobic workouts is that they don't overstress the athlete. Unfortunately, this is more often the case. Dan is a typical example.

Case History
Dan had just completed a successful winter aerobic base period and was ready for spring track work. His favorite race distance was 10K, and this year his goal was to break 40 minutes. He began his track sessions with quarter mile repeats at 75 seconds each, with a quarter mile jog in between. When race time came, his times were only a few seconds faster than the previous year. What's worse, his times got slower as the season wore on and he never came close to breaking 40 minutes.

Why was Dan doing his intervals so fast? He has not yet broken 40 minutes for 10K, so his interval pace of 75 second quarters is far beyond his racing ability. He would produce much less stress and get the same benefit if his quarters were 90 seconds. This would provide a much bigger net gain.

If we looked at Dan's heart rate, we'd get a better idea of how stressful his workout was. Running a quarter mile in 75 seconds brought Dan's heart rate to about 180. At 35 years of age, this is very close to his maximum heart rate. Running the same quarter mile at 90 seconds would bring his heart rate to about 170, closer to 90% of his max heart rate. This represents a more efficient training heart rate for an anaerobic workout.

The first simple suggestion for anaerobic work is that the your heart rate not exceed 90% of its max heart rate. This regardless of the type of workout. For example, if you're doing intervals on a track, use the heart rate as your primary guide, along with your time. On a bike, keep an eye on your heart rate more than the other riders.

My favorite recommendation for anaerobic workouts is fartlek. In addition to muscular, metabolic and neurological benefits, it also incorporates an important mental aspect of training; specifically, it forces you to become more aware of your body and its needs. For many, this style is a relief from the burden of the clock. In time, you may be able to do the whole workout by intuition and be relieved of the need to even look at your heart rate.

Keep It Short
If the duration of anaerobic workouts is excessive, it can also contribute to overtraining and ill health. So the second principle is, keep it short. This relates to both the time of each workout, and the number of weeks these workouts are maintained.

Your neurological, metabolic and muscular body has a limit on what it can gain from a given individual anaerobic workout. And I do mean limit: 45 minutes for high stress activity such as running, 60 to 90 minutes for other activities like cycling, skating and swimming. This is, however, sufficient time to get substantial benefits. And remember, these times include your warm up and cool down. So after this workout, don't expect to come home ready to collapse; it's not necessary.

How long should you continue doing the anaerobic part of your schedule? That depends on a number of factors. The biggest is stress; specifically, how much stress do you have in the rest of your life. Since stress and anaerobic work create similar metabolic states, the more stress you have the less anaerobic work you want to do.

Another important factor is time; how much time do you have, especially for recovery. It takes longer to recover from anaerobic sessions, and if your days and evenings are generally busy with other commitments, you may not have the luxury of doing much anaerobic work.

The best way to answer the question of how long you should continue anaerobic work is by performing the MAF Test. If you see a slowing of your pace at any time during your anaerobic training phase, it's time to stop and return to aerobic base training. A worsening of your MAF Test would indicate you've done too much anaerobic work. As many athletes find, only a few short weeks of anaerobic training is all that many require.

For most endurance athletes, the maximum time for anaerobic work is about 8 weeks. This is the maximum, and more of an exception. For the average endurance athlete who works a 40-hour per week job, especially if they have a family, 5 weeks may be possible. Most athletes can obtain maximum anaerobic benefits after three to four weeks. But for many, no anaerobic training is best.

By now, you're asking yourself the customary question; "How will I get fast if I don't train fast?" Let me emphasize as I did earlier, and assure you that endurance races are 95-99% aerobic. You will increase your race speed by getting more efficient through aerobic training.

Going through a yearly schedule without anaerobic work is a dramatic break from tradition. But once you've done it, and see the positive results, you'll have no trouble creating a new tradition.

Actually, you are performing some anaerobic work when you're racing. For many athletes, that's just enough hard input to keep the body balanced and working well.

Consider triathlete Mike Pigg's 1994 season – one of his best. He won most of his races and finished high up in most of the rest. He did not do any anaerobic work until mid September, when most of his races were completed.

When anaerobic training is included in your schedule, there are a few basic rules to follow:

• Including races, do not exceed 3 anaerobic workouts per week.

• For many athletes, one anaerobic workout per week is sufficient.

• Most athletes will reach maximum anaerobic benefits after 3 or 4 weeks of anaerobic work.

• The day prior to and the following day's workout should be an easy one; Never perform anaerobic workouts on two consecutive days.

• Try to mimic your race environment during anaerobic workouts. This includes running on the road, cycling with a group, or swimming open water.

• Focus on relaxation and breathing to increase your mechanical efficiency. If you're uptight and stressed, do an easy workout and try again the next day.

• Try to do your anaerobic workout in the morning, or about the same time as the start of your races.

• Be sure to warm up and cool down sufficiently.

• Treat your anaerobic workout as if it were a race; mentally and physically.

• Be sure to eat and drink enough fluid pre and post workout.

Case History
In the case of John, portrayed at the end of the last chapter, his anaerobic schedule typically looks like this:

Mon 6am – Easy 45 minute swim; 5:30pm – Easy 45 minute run.
Tues 6am – One hour swim at max aerobic heart rate; 5pm – Two hour bike: time trial.
Wed 6am – 90 minute run at max aerobic heart rate.
Thurs 6am – One hour swim at max aerobic heart rate.
Fri 6am – One hour fartlek run (anaerobic).
Sat 8am – Three hour bike; 4:30pm – Easy 45 minute swim
Sun 8am – Two hour bike (aerobic intervals) followed by on hour easy run.

John follows this schedule for about four weeks, after which he begins his racing season.

A Word about Weights
Weight lifting is anaerobic, whether you're doing low weight and high repetition, or the reverse. But don't expect to see your heart rate increase beyond your max aerobic level during a weight session; in most people, the muscle you're working fatigues before the heart rate reaches its peak level. Since you stop lifting at that point, your heart rate never reaches it's highest level. So using the heart rate to judge whether your weight workout is anaerobic is not accurate. The bottom line; weight lifting is anaerobic. So treat it that way in relation to your weekly schedule.

Weight lifting's place in endurance sports is a controversial subject when discussed by athletes, coaches and physiologists. My recommendations are usually against it, for two main reasons.

First, the average endurance athlete already has a tough schedule; training, working, family or home responsibilities, and perhaps other obligations.

Finding time for another workout – often two or three – adds stress to an often over busy week.

Second, weight workouts help the muscle, or group of muscles, to be stronger during the specific action trained during the workout. Most often, that action does not imitate the exact action during your endurance race. The result is no improvement in power during competition.

Weight lifting uses up a lot of energy during training, and builds muscle bulk. This added mass induces weight gain, sometimes significantly, which can be a negative factor during competition. In addition, in order to maintain the benefits of weight lifting, you must continue them throughout the year, if only once or twice weekly. Otherwise, most if not all of your gains will be lost.

Some feel the added muscle gained during lifting will protect them from injury. But it's the aerobic muscle fibers which perform this work much more than the anaerobic fibers built during weight training.

If your schedule permits two or three added workouts per week, and you have built as good an aerobic base as possible, you may consider weights as an added workout.

Think of all anaerobic training, including weights, as an investment; It's a high risk with a small return. Would you spend money on such a scheme? In addition, fitting these workouts into your schedule – without sacrificing aerobic benefits – may be adding yet another stress to your week. Fortunately, most endurance athletes can obtain all the anaerobic stimulation necessary from racing. And racing after building a good aerobic base results in great performances.

Chapter 12

Training Schedules for Age Group Athletes

Learning how to train for both health and fitness involves a number of factors; experience, technique, intuition, and some basic knowledge about the body. There are also some fundamental considerations about piecing your training schedule together, considering you may have an even busier job with the rest of your life's chores. By far the most important consideration is this:

First understand the primary rules of training – warm up, cool down, heart rate, etc. – and successfully apply them. Then, your day to day schedule becomes a secondary feature – exactly how many minutes per day you train is no longer the main focus. It will fall into place on it's own.

Perhaps a better title for this chapter is "Less is More." Meaning that for the average athlete with many other responsibilities, less training usually produces better athletic performance than trying to accumulate many miles and hours of training.

The majority of the athletes I have worked with in my career, like most of the readers of this book, are not professionals. If you work a full time job, perhaps have a family, a house and other responsibilities you can still train and perform at very high levels. But don't expect to be able to put in the same amount of time and miles as professional athletes. Nor do you need to for success.

Most of the time, I find that diminishing the total training hours per week allows for more recovery and less stress. This helps the aerobic system build itself much more efficiently. When race season comes, you're more refreshed and ready to race.

Case History
Carla was a back of the pack Triathlete with hopes of improving her performances. But after her fourth year of diminishing returns, she sought help with her schedule. After reading one of my earlier books, she strictly followed the program. Except for one thing; her workout schedule averaged 18 hours per week. Unfortunately, Carla really didn't have the time for that amount

of training, but she tried to squeeze in the workouts. She worked part time and had a family that included two young children.

In mid-November, I recommending she cut her schedule to about 12 hours per week. It was also the only change necessary. Carla was doing everything else right. By the end of next summer's racing season, eight out of nine races were personal bests. Carla also placed in the top five of her age group in half of those events.

For many years, scientists have know that there is a limit to how much an athlete can train before it adversely effects race performance.

The majority of your physical benefits received from training occur in the first 10 weeks of the season. Maintaining the benefits obtained in this early phase, such as VO_2 max, can be maintained very easily with much less training. One study showed that maintaining VO_2 max could be accomplished by cutting training by two-thirds!

If you train regularly, year after year, your improvement will be slower through the later years compared to early on, but you can maintain that improvement with much less effort. Additional effort will not necessarily produce more improvements.

Classic scientific studies show no evidence that in single sport activities multiple daily training sessions improve performance more than single daily sessions. Studies on swimmers demonstrated that heart rate and lactate levels, and performance times, were no different between two groups of athletes; one training twice daily and one with a single workout.

While many of these investigations are short term, longer studies provide the same information regarding training volume. Research which examined swimmers over a five year period showed those who swam 10,000 meters daily performed no different than those who trained daily at half that distance.

Despite the evidence that less training offers more benefits, endurance athletes still overtrain too often. Part of the problem may be social.

Our social trend in athletics today, especially in the U.S., is still that of "no pain, no gain." This philosophy is asserted in advertising, magazine articles, schools and has become a vicious cultural cycle. And, our very young athletes are exposed to this conviction long before they learn about being healthy and fit. In many cases, they learn about the later after it's too late.

Learning about yourself will help determine an ideal schedule. This includes commitment, time allotment, goals, etc. Applying that information to your particular sport is the next step for success.

If you are training for a single sport, your schedule is usually easier than if you are a multisport athlete. Most of the time, you'll have one workout a day. The best time to do this is based more on your daily non-training schedule; when do you work, what other obligations exist, etc. Many runners, for example, find a morning workout most suitable. Other sports have limits; swimmers usually have pool hours to consider, cyclists and skiers the weather. I frequently recommend single-sport athletes perform some other event one to three times per week. This cross training has a positive benefit, especially for the nervous system, as long as it is aerobic and fits into your schedule.

If you are a multisport athlete with two or more sports, you'll have a busier schedule. But this does not mean you have to perform each sport every day.

One luxury of being a professional is your job is to train and race. You have most, if not all of the day available to train – not that you'd workout all day. A pro Triathlete, for example, may swim an hour in the morning, go for a two-hour bike ride mid-day and run an hour in the late afternoon. But if you're an age-group athlete, this schedule usually won't work.

For those doing more than one sport, you don't have the luxury of working out in all your events each day. Nor is that required. However, many endurance athletes attempt this, sometimes no matter what the outcome.

Case History
Jay was stuck in an overtraining cycle for at least three years. He would train in each of his three events as many days as possible. He would run at five a.m., swim at noon and ride late in the day. The problem: Jay had his own business and worked from seven a.m. until nine p.m. He also had a family. Maintaining that schedule five days, with Tuesday and Thursday reserved for his long bike and run respectively, was quite a chore.

Jay would become exhausted regularly, and about every couple of months, he'd have to take a week or two off, completely. As he started feeling better, he would pick up his "normal" schedule again. I gave Jay my version of a normal program, explaining how he would race better and get more healthy. However, he could not understand how one could improve without the high mileage weeks. I never saw Jay again in the office, but occasionally would meet him at a race, where year after year he showed no improvement.

If you're a multisport athlete and get at least three days a week of each activity, your schedule can be very effective. If you attempt to do otherwise, you risk overtraining. If possible, spread these workouts through the week so they are not on consecutive days. For example:

> Swim   Monday, Wednesday, Saturday
> Bike   Tuesday, Thursday, Saturday, Sunday
> Run   Monday, Thursday, Sunday

For most athletes, the weekend can provide longer workouts. Perhaps a longer bike on Saturday and longer run Sunday. Or, you can combine two events and make one longer workout such as a two-hour bike followed by a 45 minute run. A favorite winter workout is a swim immediately followed by an hour of indoor biking on rollers or a trainer. These combined sessions provide not only a longer workout but helps mimic race transitions, where your body has to adjust to the stress of changing from one event to another.

Notice the above schedule has nothing planned for Friday. This is an off day, something most athletes don't get enough of. If you feel better calling them a rest or recovery day, go right ahead. Sometimes the word "off" refers to not doing anything. But these days provide a most important part of the training formula:

> *training = work + rest.*

I recommend at least one rest day per week to help with recovery. During the racing season, when you will more easily maintain your fitness level with less training but require more recovery, two rest days are even better. Off days are best taken going into a weekend, if that is your busiest training time or if there is a race. Another appropriate time is Monday, which is a day when a lot of your energy is needed for recovery. Or make Monday an easy day if Friday is your off day and the weekend includes a lot of training.

When planning rest days (and easy ones), consider your work stress too. If Mondays are always your busiest or hardest on the job, don't train that day.

Seasonal stress may also be a factor. If you're an accountant and your busiest time is tax season in the early spring, make that an easy training time too, and postpone your racing until early summer.

Another important time to take it easy is at the end of your training and racing year. For most northern hemisphere athletes this is November or December. At this time I recommend taking two to three weeks completely off, or more if you need it. While periods of rest are helpful for the body, a mental break is just as important. During this time just let your body do what it wants; watch TV, go for hikes, paint your house, etc.

At this point, you may be looking for me to provide a training schedule. There is none that would prove ideal for all the readers of this book. Keeping in mind all the rules – from warm up to proper heart rate to cool down – and fitting your workouts into your week where they won't stress anyone, you'll have no trouble formulating your own schedule. This is how I do in my office with any age group athlete. This is also how I do it with the pros.

Chapter 13

Training at Altitude

For many years, training at altitude has maintained a certain mystique. Cities like Boulder, Colorado have blossomed as an endurance mecca in part due to the training benefits many believe would come with working out there.

Unfortunately, spending time in Boulder is not the magic ingredient for the improved endurance many seek. Actually, more athletes who go to higher altitudes to train end up overtraining. Part of the problem is due to social factors. But even the moderate elevation of cities like Boulder increases the training heart rate for weeks. If training is based on pace rather than heart rate, most athletes end up training too hard. With the "thinner" air, overtraining often follows.

Being at altitude does come with benefits. One advantage is just living there. As a result of taking in less oxygen, the body adapts by producing more red blood cells. This is the result of the hormone erythropoietin. The higher the elevation, the more this process proceeds. In addition, the hemoglobin content in the blood increases as well, all providing an increased oxygen-carrying capacity of the blood. While these benefits are good for your health, it only improves your fitness when, and if, you return to lower altitudes to compete.

Returning to sea level, for example, three weeks before a major race offers the best of both altitudes. First, at the lower altitude your oxygen uptake is greater. And second, you maintain the improved oxygen-carrying capacity developed during your time at altitude, which helps prepare you for competition. This has been Mark Allen's strategy through the years he won his six Hawaiian Ironman races.

Another benefit of training at altitude is not a physiological one. The enjoyment of being in most moderate level mountainous regions is socially and psychologically rewarding. Whether in the Rocky Mountains, in the ranges of the southwest or the northwest corridor, most areas offer a healthy, low stress place to train and live compared to hurried, tension-ridden areas such as New York or Los Angeles. And, the summer weather in these mountain areas offer additional benefits of being less humid and cooler; a radical change from places like Atlanta, Florida and Texas.

Let's look at more of the changes that occur when training at altitude.

The air you breath at higher altitudes is the same as the air at sea level; it contains about 21% oxygen. The barometric pressure, however, is lower as you ascend in altitude, and the difference creates a decreased ability to get oxygen out of the air.

In addition to oxygen changes, altitude training also imposes other factors that must be considered. Temperature, humidity and solar radiation are the most important.

As you ascend, air temperature drops at a rate of about 1 degree C for every 150 meters. This can be significant when cycling to higher elevations, especially when considering the wind chill. Humidity is also much lower at higher altitudes, since cold air holds much less water. Water loss is increased, from respiratory evaporation, due to increased respiration and from water loss through sweating. This poses a potential problem of dehydration, an already frequent dilemma in athletes.

You should also be aware of the solar danger at higher altitude. Because there is less air for the light to travel through, more of it reaches you. In addition, the decreased water in the air, which normally absorbs light, also increases the amount of light that hits your body. And if there is snow, reflective light can amplify this problem as well.

The muscles are also effected by altitude and have difficulty adjusting as well. In general, this is a problem beginning with altitudes above about 1,600 meters (5,248 feet). In this situation, muscle performance is greatly diminished due to the rapid decline of VO_2 max. In addition, muscle enzymes, which regulate energy production, decline, and total surface area of the muscle also is diminished.

One important fact about altitude training is that we don't know everything about it. This leaves empirical information – the observation of what seems to work best – along with the scientific information that is useful.

Here are some of my recommendations for those who want to travel to altitude to train for endurance.

• The ideal altitude for endurance training is between 1,500 meters and 2,000 meters.

- If you plan to stay at altitude for long periods (such as the summer months), your training should be diminished for the first two weeks of arriving at altitude. For the first two or three days, training should be restricted to easy walking.

- Anaerobic workouts should be minimized while training at altitude.

- If competing at altitude, train aerobically for at least two weeks at that altitude in order to adapt.

- If you are not able to stay at altitude for two weeks before competition, arrive at your race the night before. Many of the negative physiological changes become significant after the first 24 hours at altitude.

Perhaps the best recommendation I could make is that if you have the option to train any place you like, chose a location which is most pleasant to live. A more relaxed environment with good weather will do more for you than anything else.

Chapter 14

Racing: Preparation, Implementation & Recovery

For most athletes, this is what it's all about; the race. It should not only be rewarding and fun, but educational. Racing is the culmination of all your discipline, the end result of your labor. But for too many, it's a time of disappointment. For racing success, three important actions must be effectively executed; preparation, implementation and recovery. These factors should help you answer the question, are you ready to race?

Preparation

There are two important aspects of preparation. The first is tapering, and the second is knowing when your body is ready to race.

Tapering is a period of diminished training. It enables your body to rest and recover from the training that hopefully has been successful. Even though you are working out much less, this period of reduced activity should not take away from your race performance, but rather enhance it by assuring you are well rested for race day.

The routines I have used for years, which are supported by the published research of others, indicate that at least two weeks of tapering is optimal for long events like a marathon, a cycling tour or an Ironman. Even for shorter events, a few days of tapering can make a significant difference in performance.

During the taper period, reduce your training by 50-80%; with less training as you get closer to race day. In addition, avoid all anaerobic training during the taper period. Downhill runs or spinning on your bike can help the nervous system maintain its turnover capability.

The scientific literature shows that during a taper period your muscle strength actually increases. In addition, no reduction in VO_2 max or MAF occurs.

In a study using runners, a 60% reduction in training for 15 to 21 days showed no loss in either endurance or VO_2 max.

Another benefit of tapering is that the rest significantly improves leg power; improved arm strength in swimmers has also been noted in studies. Other benefits include lower lactate levels once competition begins.

Tapering must be differentiated from detraining, which is the complete cessation of working out. With no training, endurance is adversely effected after only two weeks.

The second aspect of preparation is knowing when your body is ready to race. You can determine this using three methods:

 1. The first and most effective is through information obtained from your MAF Test.

 2. The second and most common is by the calendar.

 3. The third and most dangerous is because everyone else is doing it.

The MAF Test Analysis
The most effective way to determine the ideal time to start racing is to assess your body. This is best accomplished by the MAF Test.

Building your aerobic base is the most important aspect of training, and the most significant factor in racing. So before embarking on competition, allow your body to build as much aerobic function as possible. An improvement in your aerobic speed and a natural plateau may indicate you've reached your maximum aerobic benefits for that base period.

Can competition be successful having only trained aerobically for up to several months? The answer is not only yes, but you can more often race your best following a good aerobic base period.

Recall that endurance events are 95% or more aerobic in nature. This much aerobic requirement for racing may be part of the reason for the results in a clinical study I did in the early to mid 1980s. I found more than 75% of the runners I trained over a four year period raced personal bests in their spring races following a winter aerobic base. The key point of this survey was to show that a majority of runners could run well without anaerobic training.

For many endurance athletes, the ideal approach is to build a big base, typically in the winter, and start racing in the spring. Let the racing satisfy any need for anaerobic stimulation. This keeps your training schedule more stress free, allows for more racing, and further assures you don't overtrain.

Case History
Charlie was racing better each of the last 6 years. Now at age 36, and in a new age group, he decided to continue the same strategy that was successful. He built a good winter base by only training aerobically. In the spring, he would begin road racing and duathlons as his tune up for the summer triathlons. As the season progressed, so did his racing. And each year his times for the same races improved over the previous year.

The Calendar Method
Just because it's April doesn't mean you have to race. Don't let the calendar dictate your training and racing patterns; it may not correlate with your body's readiness.

If you want to race at a certain time of year, make sure you're prepared by allowing enough time to build an aerobic base.

If you race too early in your training calendar, or too much throughout it, racing is frequently a frustrating and depressing experience.

The Go-With-The-Flow Method
Unfortunately, too many athletes don't plan their races. They allow others to do that, by following what the crowd does.

Be your own athlete. And plan your season well ahead of time.

Racing should also be more than a casual, social event you jump into because you've got little else to do on a Sunday.

Obviously, the best way to determine race readiness is through objective assessment, such as with the MAF Test. In addition, there are other factors to consider when beginning to make that transition from training to racing:

Resting Heart Rate
The resting heart rate is one of the standby traditional biofeedback readings we've used for decades to help assess our fitness. In the course of training, the resting heart rate normally lowers, the result of increased cardiac efficiency. If we have a cold or other stress looming over us, that resting rate increases a few or more beats reflecting the stress. So, if your rate is down over the previous couple of months, it may indicate race readiness.

However, the resting heart rate is not meant to be used exclusively as an indicator for anything, as doing that can mislead you. A case in point is during overtraining; your resting rate may actually diminish, making it appear like you're doing well. Without other indicators, you can easily be misled.

Weight & Body Fat
Many athletes gain weight over the winter, due to either less training, the wrong foods or both. As we get into better shape, that weight usually drops. But what do the numbers on the scale really tell you?

Scale weight only tells you how many pounds you weigh, and not how much fat you have stored. Your lean body mass, mostly muscle, weighs much more than an equal volume of body fat. But fat takes up much more space than an equal weight of muscle. So, if you want to know about body fat, you need to measure it separate from your lean body mass.

Calipers, water tanks and electronic gadgets may provide you with fairly accurate information about your percent body fat. But, since fat takes up space and when you lose it you get thinner, it's easier and cheaper to just measure yourself with a tape measure – although you won't get a percentage. And maybe nearly as accurate, just ask yourself, do your pants that fit so well last October fit the same now?

The reason weight and body fat are indicators of your readiness to race is twofold; first, if your body weight is too high for your frame, it may make for a slower swim, bike or run. That's due to more gravity stress and drag, not to mention that more oxygen is required. But it does not mean the thinner you are the faster you'll be. Like everything else in life, the extremes are dangerous. If you're too thin and have lost too much lean body mass, you'll have less muscle to burn fat and power you through your events. And, if you have too little fat stored, your energy and hormonal systems – and protective padding – may be jeopardized.

The ideal, of course, is not to gain weight in the winter. So, if your program is effective, your weight and fat content will come down to "normal." If this is the case, it's likely you're ready to race.

Your Diary
We all have a story to tell. And part of yours is written in your diary – if you keep one. Like any story, you often have a good idea what may happen next. Is it time to race? Read your diary.

Your diary might include everything from total time and heart rates of each workout, which course you took that day and how far you went. It may mention the weather, how you felt, along with your fears and dreams.

Looking back over the past few months in your diary, you can more objectively assess your progress. Look for consistency, and gradual increases in total time of each workout, indicating increased fitness.

Mental Readiness
As your diary pages fill, your training enjoyment should too. Note how you've felt along the way. For example, as your rides become longer, were they still playful? Is your long run leaving you with a more positive feeling about training? With this type of analysis, you'll more easily see your readiness – or disinclination – to race.

Also, and even more subjective, is your intuition. As you derive benefits from training, you should not only get more fit, but healthy. And, as you build both your mental and physical health, you may find it easier to answer the question; Are you ready to race?

Blood Chemistry
There is a chemical part of you that must also be ready to race. The minerals, proteins and enzymes which keep your aerobic engine running smooth must be balanced before embarking on your season.

The best and easiest way to generally evaluate this component is a blood test. This can be done at a local laboratory, although you'll probably need an order from your doctor.

Individual labs may use different names for certain tests, but there are some essential items you'll want checked. In addition, your doctor may want additional tests per your specific needs. Below is a list of the basics:

1. CBC with indices. This Complete Blood Count measures the red blood cells, along with the hemoglobin, hematocrit and other associated factors. The white blood cells are also counted, with the percentage of each cell listed along with other factors.

2. Blood Chemistry. This common test is actually a measurement of many different elements in the blood. From sugar (glucose) to proteins, minerals (calcium, iron, sodium and potassium) to fats (total cholesterol and

triglycerides), and others. In all, there are at least 24 items this test measures, (some labs do the shorter version, which I don't recommend). This test should be done in the fasting state – no food or liquid (other than water) for 12 hours. So the best time to get the test done is first thing in the morning after not eating all night.

3. Miscellaneous Tests. If the blood chemistry test above did not measure some key items, have them done in addition. Here are some examples; Without your HDL and LDL cholesterol, the total cholesterol (measured above) provides little information. The amount of iron in your blood (serum iron) and in your red blood cells (hemoglobin) is important, but so is the amount stored. This stored iron is called ferritin, and can be tested separately. If you have too little or too much ferritin, there could be problems; too little means there's not enough iron to take the place of what you loose (especially in sweat). Too much means, potentially, you could increase unwanted free radical chemicals which contribute to inflammation and other unpleasant conditions. (That's why taking iron supplements when it's not indicated can be dangerous.)

All these tests will require at least two tubes of blood to be drawn – not a significant loss during training. However, it's not recommend taking the test right before a race.

The so-called "normal" levels are spelled out on the test result sheet. But laboratory "normals" are made, in part, from the average of the population, which gives you a very wide range. I prefer a more narrow range. Some doctors are aware of this factor and can help you with the right interpretation.

In general, however, blood tests are just a ruling out process. They will tell you if there is any significant problem, such as anemia (iron deficiency) or hyperlipoproteinemia (high blood fats called triglycerides). But you could have a normal iron level and still have a nutritional need for iron, or normal triglycerides and still be storing them on your hips or in your arteries. Other comprehensive tests including a good history can give clues about these problems.

Pre-Race Practices
A significant part of racing is your pre-race routine: the habits you adopt the few days before your event.

It's Thursday, and you're getting ready for Sunday's race. Your habits over the next few days can make a dramatic difference in your race performance, and how well you recovery.

Sometimes even subtle stresses can have significant effects on your race performance. Being aware of the most important ones, and making the appropriate adjustments can assist with a more efficient and enjoyable race day.

Below are the most common mistakes I've seen athletes make in the days leading up to their race, and especially on race day.

1. Perhaps the most common nutritional deficiency in athletes is water. Dehydration may increase with pre-race stress and especially hot weather. Athletes are too often dehydrated, with the problem more prevalent in the days before a race.

The best way to remain hydrated is to drink small amounts of water – two to six ounces each time – throughout the day and evening, rather than a couple of high volume loads here and there. Carry a water bottle around with you during the days before your race, and on race morning.

2. Stay out of the sun during the days prior to the race. You'll dehydrate more quickly in the sun. In addition – and even more important – the sun increases body stress which will have an adverse effect on your performance. So stay in the shade as much as possible. If you must go out in the sun, wear a hat and light clothing that covers you.

3. Keep your workouts to a minimum, if at all, in both duration and intensity. The best rule regarding training the week of the race, especially the few days before; less is best. You'll receive no race benefits by training during these last few days. However, you want to keep loose, and too little activity can make you stiff and jittery. So, if you feel you want to workout, some short, easy bouts are ideal, but keep it to a minimum. And the day or two right before the race you should consider taking off completely, using walking to stay loose. (See "tapering" below for more specifics.)

4. While most athletes ponder the power behind their muscles, they usually underestimate the power of the mind. But you can train it just like your muscles. You have control over some potentially stressful activity before you race; how you think. Negative thoughts about the race can and should be turned into a positive outlook with realistic aspirations. You are

in charge of your mind, but traditions, past experiences (yours and other peoples) and other memories have major influences. So remember, you're there to have fun and perform the best you can.

5. Continue to eat the same kinds of food you're used to – assuming you're on the right diet for your needs. Also try to stay on the same time schedule. Late night dinners with foods – and alcohol – you don't usually consume can potentially be dangerous to your performance. Remember, the body doesn't like too much change.

6. Follow the same race routine that has proven to work for you; assuming it's a healthy one. If you're not sure what works, pay more attention to your body. Don't just blindly copy what others do. Avoid trying new bike equipment, running shoes, drinks and food during the race. Experiment during training, not on race day.

7. Warm up on race morning. Depending on the distance and race layout, you can walk, swim, run easy or all three. If you have an adequate aerobic base, a good warm up should total at least about 20-30 minutes for most shorter races. If you don't have a good aerobic base, you may not be ready to race.

8. Eating on race morning is very individual. Experiment during a hard training workout or a low key race to determine what works best. For many athletes, drinks or bars work very well in place of a meal. However, avoid high sugar foods and drinks since these will adversely affect fat burning during the race.

Implementation
Racing is an experience. The more you do it the more successful you will be, given all other factors being equal.

There are so many specific factors relating to each type of race, and other aspects relevant to distance, intensity, altitude, weather, etc. However, there are some key factors which can make a significant difference in your race result.

Whether you're competing in a 5K or a 6-day running race, a long bike tour or short road race, or swimming the English Channel, the first rule of racing is, don't go out too fast. This forces your body to burn more sugar, running the risk of depleting your glycogen stores early, which will cause your fat burning to diminish too.

Starting some races at a comfortable pace, perhaps just faster than your average speed for the race, is the most practical solution. It may take discipline to avoid getting caught up with the pack – most of whom will go out too hard. But don't worry, you'll pass them later in the race. This may not always work in cycling – more of a reason to warm up well.

For some events going out slower for the first part of the race works even better. You'll build your speed throughout and finish very strong. In this instance, athletes often say it's the most fun they've had racing.

Another important component of the racing is learning how to relax. The start of any event can have you over anxious and gripped with tension. Just think about standing there waiting for the start. Your heart rate is high, you're tense, and breathing is fast and shallow. While some of this energy is important for the race, much of it is an overstatement by the mind and a drain of energy.

From the moments before the race starts, focus on your breathing and relaxation. If you're successful at this, your form will be better, you'll have a lower heart rate and your times will improve – all from being more efficient.

Perhaps you require a physical focus on race day; write the word "breath" or "relax" on you hand or arm where you can easily see it. Or tell yourself that whenever you see a yellow line (on the road), water, or any visual cue, your body will breath and relax properly (a technique used in hypnosis).

Another successful strategy is to avoid high peaks in your heart rate during the race. This can only be done if you're using a heart rate monitor.

The heart rate normally increases when you are ascending a hill or speeding up, sometimes dramatically. For example, you may be riding along on the road averaging 150 heart rate, when suddenly you begin to climb a steep grade. Your heart rate can also climb as well, sometimes to 170, 180 or to its maximum level.

In a shorter event, this poses less of a problem. But in longer races it can have devastating effects on your energy, using up too much sugar and glycogen. If this is done too early in a long event – even one lasting only an hour or two – you may risk running out of fuel later in the race.

That doesn't mean you should let the pack out of your sight or slow to a crawl at every hill. If you've built enough aerobic speed you'll be able to ascend hills at a good pace without the heart rate rising to maximum levels.

However, in some long events, like the Ironman, riding at your aerobic maximum heart rate and never higher during the bike portion is essential to maintain sufficient energy and still have enough left for an effective marathon.

For runners, a potential loss of energy during a race comes from over-striding. For some reason, when fatigue builds many athletes want to reach out with their legs, as if they'll go farther with the same energy. Instead, as you stride longer your body uses more energy as indicated by a higher heart rate. The best recommendation is to allow your stride length to be governed by your body and its energy levels rather than by your image of what you should look like.

Another common problem encountered by competitors during or just prior to a race is experimentation. Some even decide in the middle of a race to change their routine. That's fine if the purpose of your race is to experiment, whether it's different gears or bike set up, new running shoes or a novel race strategy.

Although all of the above items are very important in the implementation of your race, the most important issue during a race is hydration. Consider the fact that by the end of an endurance event, most athletes are dehydrated to the point where it adversely effects performance. So the simple action of drinking water is vital for a good race. The best rule is: drink as much as you can.

Recovery
Successful racing does not end at the finish line, even by winning. The final step – recovery – enables your body to "heal" from the race, obtain benefits, and prepare you for the resumption of training. Recovery is also the first step in preparation for your next race.

Recovery involves the physical, chemical and mental aspects of your body. Of the two forms – active and passive recovery – the active type is preferred for the endurance athlete and is discussed here. (Passive recovery is reserved for more severe or first aid situations, or for competitive intensities that are very low, such as golf.)

One of the significant benefits of a proper recovery is the ability to speed the reduction of blood lactate to normal levels. This occurs while blood is circulated through the liver which breaks down lactate. While this normalization of blood lactate occurs relatively quick under either type of recovery – within about two hours of competition – the sooner it is accomplished the faster you will return to a normal chemical state. The added benefit is that some of your lactate will convert to energy faster.

One problem with moderate or high levels of lactic acid in the muscle is that it changes pH – the acid/base balance. In this state, the body becomes too acid, which can impair energy production and adversely effect muscle contractility. Correction of this acid-base imbalance is accomplished by the breathing mechanism (through increased breathing rate which speeds carbon dioxide elimination). Natural bicarbonate in the blood also helps counter the increased acidity, assisted by hemoglobin and blood proteins. The kidneys also play a major role in acid-base balance.

The first phase of race recovery is your cool down. Walking, easy jogging or spinning, or swimming is a very effective way to aid recovery. 15 to 20 minutes is usually enough for most events. Intensity should be very low; do not exceed about 70% of your aerobic maximum heart rate. For example, if you're max aerobic rate is 140, your recovery heart rate should not exceed about 100, but can be below this level. This can be done immediately following the race, or you can wait until you hydrate and consume some nutrients. Be sure to wear your heart rate to assure you're not over-cooling down. It's often more difficult to gauge body intensity following a hard effort.

In some long events, such as an Ironman distance, even a few minutes of walking – sometimes in a pool – can be very therapeutic and speed recovery.

In the evening of the race, another short walk, easy spin or swim can also greatly speed recovery.

Walking is especially helpful if you have a long trip home – when you may be sitting for some time. If you're on a plane, walk at the airport and on the plane. If you have an extended drive, stop to take a walking break.

Getting into cool or cold water is also a very good therapy for recovery. It assists in the healing of over-taxed muscles and other soft tissues by increasing circulation and cooling otherwise overheated areas. A local stream, lake or even bath can work wonders, even if for only five minutes.

Post race food and drink is also important for recovery. Many people can speed glycogen replacement by drinking about 80 grams of liquid carbohydrate within 15 minutes following competition. But be sure to drink plenty of additional water with it.

No matter how much you consumed during the race, you're probably still dehydrated, and will remain so for 24 hours or more. Avoid alcohol which increases dehydration until you have consumed lots of water and eaten a meal. Salty foods or drinks with sodium are also important and will help replace the often large amounts of sodium lost in sweat, especially following long events.

The day after your race is an especially important time for recovery. Perhaps an easy swim or walk in the morning, or an easy spin or swim later in the day. No hard or long workouts. If you recover well by the end of the day after a Sunday race, you can resume normal training on Tuesday. In the case of a long event like an Ironman or long bike tour, it will take many more days to recover. Allow your body all the time it needs.

If you're ready to race, successfully following proper preparation, implementation and recovery procedures will assure you of success.

What if you're not ready to race? Don't. You'll have to sacrifice at least part of the season and get back on track. Modify and correct your training, diet or whatever needs improvement, until you are ready.

Case History

Steve came to me with chronic injuries accompanied by a variety of other overtraining symptoms. Since it was now early May, his main concern was the start of the racing season. But my consideration was for Steve's health. So the season, I explained, had to be modified. We had to correct his injuries and start building a base, which would take three months. If all went well, the plan was to start racing in July. Everything did go well, and Steve had some of his best racing ever from mid July through early October.

Chapter 15

Traveling To Your Race

If you're flying to your race, there are specific factors related to preparation that you may want to consider.

While short airline flights are not too stressful, longer excursions can beat up your body and mind. Here are some basic tips for air travelers to help overcome the strain – which may have an adverse effect on your race.

- Eat a good meal before going to the airport. And, pack some food too. Just pretend you're going on a picnic. You may not get any other acceptable food for some time.

- Arrive at the airport early to avoid the crowds, long lines and stressed people – it could wear off on you. Use the extra time to relax, read the paper or go for a walk.

- If you're looking for leg room, get a bulk-head or exit row seat. But if you don't check in early, they'll all be taken.

- While waiting for your flight, remain in a secluded area – like an empty gate lounge – to avoid annoying or stressed people, and their germs.

- Stay on your feet while waiting for boarding – you may be sitting for some time.

- Drink water throughout your trip. The low humidity in the plane's cabin dehydrates you quickly. Bring water with you. Hot tea (herbal – bring your own bags) works best because it helps humidify your sinuses.

- Avoid coffee, tea, soda and other beverages with caffeine which speeds dehydration. Alcohol also dehydrates you quickly in a low pressure cabin.

- When making connecting flights, spend some time walking around to keep loose. This will be easier if your carry-on has wheels.

- Walking around at the airport will be more convenient if you check your bags (but always carry your personal items and a change of clothing just in case your luggage gets lost). Also, try to get outside in the (fresh?) air. This is easier if you check your carry-ons into an airport locker.

- On long flights, give yourself a hand and foot massage.

- On long flights, especially to important races where rest is a priority, use your frequent flyer miles to upgrade to first class (or business, if available). Or purchase a first or business class seat. This will make your trip less of a burden because the seats are bigger with more leg room, the food is much better, and there are less lines. But the bottom line is you're treated better and you'll arrive less stressed, ready to race.

Chapter 16

Making Your Own Race Season

In many endurance sports, racing has become an around the year event. Runners, for example, can find a race within a short drive of home just about any time of year. Fortunately, for many others, seasons are restricted, mostly due to the weather. But even in this case, the race season is often a long one, with many races crammed into it. And still other situations exist; if you're a pro, you just pick up your gear and head south, or north, when the weather changes and you're in a different environment and a new race season.

Whatever your situation, at some point you'll need to make your own racing schedule. All it takes is a little planning and discipline.

If you live in cooler areas, where autumn is the end of many race seasons, the weather does half your job of scheduling. In the northeast U.S., for example, most race seasons begin with the onset of nice weather – usually April or May. The competitions continue until the cool temperatures begin, usually around the end of October.

This race season, from mid spring to mid autumn can be about five months. That's too long for any endurance athlete to maintain health and race well throughout. So breaking up this time frame is the next consideration. The best and simplest way to this is to take a break from racing in the middle of the season; essentially, breaking up your race year into two seasons.

Your first season is from April/May through June or mid-July, and your second season begins mid to late August through October. Adjust this to your specific race dates. But the most important aspect is your mid summer break.

This mid summer period is a time to build another aerobic base. It's short but sufficient to not only develop more aerobic function, but it provides you with sufficient rest and recovery so you can have a better second season. And for many sports, that late summer/autumn schedule has more important races.

The mid summer aerobic base should be no less than about four weeks, with six or eight being reserved if the race schedule is very busy. The more races in the first season the more time you need to recover. And, the more important the second season is to you the more added base you'll need.

> **Case History**
> *Sue is a triathlete who ends her race year with the Ironman in Hawaii. Here is her typical schedule:*
>
> *Winter base continues through mid-April*
> *Last two weekends in April – short running race (10K, 5K)*
> *Three weekends in May – duathlons*
> *Three weekends in June – triathlons (last one being a half Ironman)*
> *July to mid August aerobic base*
> *Last two weeks in August – triathlons*
> *Early September – half marathon running race*
> *Mid October – Ironman race*
>
> *Sue may also compete in a couple of running races in mid-November before beginning her long winter base.*

If you live in Australia or New Zealand, the Caribbean or Hawaii, or even Alaska, you can make your own schedule to match the local weather, the races and your own life. And if you're fortunate enough to move with the seasons, you can still do the same. Just don't try to have too much racing in the U.S. – spring through fall, and then more in Australia – spring through fall (while the U.S. has it's fall through winter).

In general, if you rely on racing to get your anaerobic stimulation, you can race a little more. In other words, if you perform anaerobic workouts you can't race as often without creating excess stress.

One important consideration regarding your race schedule is the weather extremes. In Arizona, for example, there may not be as many races or you may not want to race as much in the summer. During this time, even morning temperatures can be in the 90s or 100s.

If you're racing locally, you may want to use the summer as your long base period. In this case, break up your winter into two seasons. One problem with this is the case where you may want to travel north for one or two big races. These are usually held in the summer, and if that's your base time you may not want to race then.

If you've built at least one good long base (i.e. December through March), had a good racing season, and stayed healthy you may want to consider some added races in the off season. This is an exception to the rules discussed earlier. During your next long base period you can race occasionally – perhaps once or twice – without ill effects. Let me repeat the criteria:

1. You've already built at least one long base period.
2. You had a good race season
3. You were healthy throughout both base and race season. This means you performed well and did not get injured or run down.

If this is the case, racing once or twice during your long winter base (as opposed to the short summer one) should not take away from your health or fitness. And, you should be able to race extremely well.

Chapter 17

Anatomy Of An Injury

Every athlete's worse nightmare is an injury. Most of us have grown up with a very simplistic view of an injury; you over work part of your body and it gets hurt. Or, you feel being injured is part of the game. In endurance sports, that's not so.

For the endurance athlete, an injury should never happen. The only exception is trauma, where you've crashed your bike or twisted your ankle. But in this sport, injuries are not part of the game like contact events. Most important, having an injury means you've done something wrong; training, diet, nutrition, stress, etc.

Let's dissect an injury; find out where it came from and how it got there.

Athletic impairment can be described as three basic types: mechanical, chemical and mental injuries. While they overlap most of the time, for illustration I will discuss each separately.

The Mechanical Injury

You awaken for your morning workout, and as you bend to get into your shoes you feel a little twinge in your right hamstrings. Nothing more than that. But several days later, there it is again, now a bit more prominent. And that evening, the twinge turned annoyance is now beginning to be painful. The next day's workout is hindered, and by the following week, real pain. Now your hip doesn't seem to move right and your knee is throbbing. After another week, all the pain has settled around the knee. You recall no trauma, your shoes are good, and you've not changed training routines.

This "domino effect" takes place in millions of athletes throughout the world. An injury; beginning from some seemingly benign event and evolving into real impairment. But there's logic to your body. Events are not random happenings. As Einstein said, "God doesn't play dice." An injury is, with some exceptions, simply an end result of a series of dominos falling over; one little, innocuous problem effecting something else, and so on. The end result is, sometimes after a half dozen or so dominos have fallen, a symptom. Pain, dysfunction, loss of power, all depending on how the body adapts and compensates to the falling dominos.Let's go back to our "typical" injury, and use the one above; knee pain. This is one of the most common athletic injuries. From a professional standpoint, there are two views when confronted with our knee problem.

The traditional view, and in recent decades the more popular approach, attempts to name the condition; if the pain is more lateral and especially a bit above the knee joint, it may be called "ilio-tibial band syndrome." If just below the knee and especially in a younger athlete it may be called "Osgood-Schlatter." And if the pain is more medial, perhaps it's referred to as a meniscus tear. This senseless attempt to name the symptoms tells nothing of how the problem occurred, how to fix the problem, and how to prevent it from returning once it is corrected.

This approach also assumes each "bursitis" is exactly the same, or every "tendinitis" is identical. And, modern medicine has an off the shelf treatment for each name; from rest to stretching, heat to cold, from anti-inflammatory drugs to surgery.

The most indefensible aspect of this cook-book approach is the fact that many professionals know what they're going to do to you before they even see you. Look up the name of your problem in the medical books and you'll find your remedy. It's a classic case of treating the symptom and ignoring the cause – and the athlete attached.

The alternative view is to look at the whole athlete. And, much like Sherlock Holmes, piece together the circumstances that led to the big event, the symptom. These clues provide vital information on how the problem was created and therefore how to avoid it in the future, and how to correct the real cause of the problem. With this approach, each injury is seen as part of the athlete. And each athlete as a unique individual with specific needs; those most appropriate for his or her precise condition. Anything less is an insult to the human body.

So just how does the symptom of knee pain evolve. Of course, our example is just one athlete's paradigm. The same knee pain in a dozen athletes could easily have different patterns. But let this one serve as one example, taking away the over-simplified view and replace it with a real life scenario.

Our athlete awakens one morning, puts on his shoes for a workout and feels the first symptom; a twinge in the hamstring muscles. But this is not the beginning of the problem. The first domino fell, perhaps, long before this first manifestation, possible months earlier.

Like an unsuspecting butler, perhaps it was the left foot – the opposite side of the eventual symptomatic knee – that underwent micro-trauma due to the training shoe not fitting properly. This is a common problem which results in biomechanical stress in the foot and ankle. While this produced no symptoms, it did effect, in a very adverse way, the mechanics of the left ankle. As is often the case when there is this type of mechanical stress on the body, the brain senses the problem and attempts to adapt. In this case, perhaps compensation takes place through the bones and muscles in the pelvis. Specifically, the pelvis tilted to modify it's movement so that weight bearing decreased on the side of stress, and increased on the opposite side – where our symptom will eventually take place. But not yet.

The increased weight bearing on the right side – usually measurable by standing on two scales – may cause some of the muscles in the thigh to become overworked. This is also partly due to the gait change resulting from the tilt in the pelvis. This causes a right "short leg," another commonly named symptom used often. Due to the mechanical stress in the pelvis, the quadriceps muscles may, through an unsuccessful attempt at compensation, become weaker or inhibited. And finally, the opposite muscles – the hamstrings – compensate to the quad problem by tightening.

Bending forward to put on your right shoe requires the hamstrings to stretch. But when they are too tight and you ask them to do their job anyway, they could become overstretched with slight micro-tears. This is the form of that slight twinge.

So what could we propose as therapy in our knee-pained athlete? Anti-inflammatory drugs? Ice the knee? The answer is obvious now that the whole picture is apparent. Find and fix the cause of the problem. In our case here, the first domino to fall was a shoe that was not right for the foot that went into it. (This doesn't mean that all knee problems are the result of shoes.) Whether all the dominos will line up on their own if you pick up the first one depends on the athlete and how much damage was done. Generally, the body has a great natural ability to heal itself. And in many cases, this is just what takes place when the cause of the problem is corrected.

This is the meaning of prevention. How can you avert problems before they begin? Consider that many athletes, when questioned about their injury, often comment about clues such as their shoes may not fit. It may be a passing thought – a subconscious note. But it's there. And most athletes possess this ability, but unfortunately most also ignore or can't read it. Learning how to read your body is worth the effort and comes in time.

More importantly, when your body gives you a very obvious sign – a hamstring twinge – it's time to STOP. Assess what's going on or it may quickly be too late. Waiting until you're physically unable to train – the point where your body forces you to stop – just results in more time wasted and unnecessary damage.

And finally, consider that this whole process, from the time the first domino fell, may take weeks or months, and in some cases years. And throughout this entire process, your performance is adversely effected.

The Chemical Injury
You spend most of your spare time training, and you're juggling work and family/social life with your sport. Going for a ride is as common as going to bed at night. But now it's getting harder to get through the day due to fatigue. And, training no longer energizes you. You're more irritable than ever. The few pounds you've gained, the first in some time, is probably due to the ravenous appetite you recently acquired. And you're on the forth cold in six months. If you could only sleep as well as you used to. "Luckily I'm not injured," you tell your training partners.

Well, my friend, you are injured. No, not the usual type of mechanical impairment we're most familiar with – such as knee pain. This is a chemical injury.

Chemical injuries typically don't produce the pains like their mechanical counterpart. Although some may provide symptoms of inflammation which can be painful. More often, and by far the most common characteristic of a chemical problem, is it makes you tired. Either the cause of the problem, or the fatigue itself, may in turn produce other chemical symptoms like the ones just described.

As we did above, let's look at the options open to the athlete with these symptoms. Here is the evidence: fatigue, irritability, increased weight gain and hunger, colds and insomnia.

As with any injury, the first step is to rule out more serious conditions – anemia, infections, or other disorders. This is often easily done with the right blood tests, and the proper history and physical exam. And when the lab report is found normal, we've taken the first step in the right direction. Genuine diseases most likely don't exist.

Once diseases are ruled out, more conservative methods – as opposed to extreme measures – can be considered. But wait, we must consider whether our patient is making all this up in his head. Is it an emotional memory he's having related to a past experience? An unpleasant episode with training wheels as a young lad? Let's conclude this is not the case.

Our athlete, who has compiled an inventory of symptoms which is having an adverse outcome on his lifestyle, usually has a common chemical scenario of cause and effect.

Perhaps the problem originated when the schedule – not just the training log, but all of life's time commitments – got too full. A key word above – the actual one used by the athlete – gives a vital clue; juggling. Our athlete was squeezing into his schedule all the items of the day, including the training. For many, this offends the body's ability to properly recover. And as the months went by, a recuperative deficit built up. Perhaps a better word is stress. The body has a system designed to adapt and compensate for all this stress; The adrenals.

So, let me piece together the possible events leading to the athlete's chemical injury. Perhaps it was some early success in racing that lead our athlete to increase his training. Undoubtedly, total workout times were not only increased, but so was the intensity. With that, the added stress of rushing the meals, and dashing from home to work, workout to home, etc. You know what I mean.

Initially, the increased stress was tolerated well by the adrenal glands. After all, that's their job. But like a long event you're not trained for, the vicious cycle of work, family and social life, training and racing got faster and more difficult to keep pace. Soon, there was less time to do the things that needed to get done, and recovery was hindered. And because you attempt to keep up with your schedule, eventually your adrenal glands became less effective at dealing with all the stress. At this point, recovery may come to a halt.

With the adrenals not able to keep up, the bodily functions it maintains begin to decline. The blood sugar becomes more unstable, which may produce symptoms of fatigue. Also, as the brain is deprived of the sugar it needs, cravings and increased hunger follows. And not only is the brain sensitive to relatively small changes in blood sugar, but the whole nervous system. As such, irritability may follow.

Because of the influence the adrenal glands have on other hormone systems of the body, we may find our athlete's metabolism falling. With this may come a shift in fuel usage: more sugar and less fat. This can result in more stored fat, and often decreased endurance. Now our athlete has to work harder to keep pace even in training. And race results become even more frustrating. Inevitably, hunger intensifies and fatigue worsens.

Excess adrenal stress is frequently accompanied by decreased immunity. With our body defense system suppressed, colds and flu, and even allergies become more common, and chronic.

And finally, falling off to sleep may be easy, since fatigue often turns to exhaustion in the early evening. But in many with excess adrenal stress, cortisol – one substance that's overproduced – oddly wakens the person in the middle of the night full of the wrong energy, and falling back to sleep becomes difficult.

Like any problem we encounter, correction first involves finding the origin. While many therapies may help remedy the symptoms, the real cause may linger unless it is dealt with. After all, a symptom is, by definition, just some evidence – and you don't want to treat your evidence, you want to address the cause.

For example, nutritional support for our athlete might include everything from Vitamin A for the immune system to zinc for the adrenals. But if the lifestyle schedule, which may have created the original stress, is not modified, problems can continually recur somewhere in the person's chemistry – as either the same set of symptoms or a gathering of new ones.

This is a typical scenario of a chemically injured athlete. It began innocently enough with a busy schedule, which chemically overtaxed an unsuspecting adrenal system. It continued by producing fatigue, hunger, irritability and colds.

For some, however, this common primary chemical problem may lead to secondary mechanical symptoms, a different cause but much like the symptoms portrayed in the mechanical example above. Unfortunately, these end-result symptoms, secondary to chemical stress, are often seen as the chief problem because they are most apparent. That is why many therapies don't work on a given individual – the real problem is never found and the body can not heal.

For others less fortunate, the chemical injury may also trigger an impairment on a mental level.

The Mental Injury
When we think of mental problems, visions of psychological tension and emotional instability come to mind. But we should distinguish the mental state from the psychological; and realize that many athletes struggle with mental distress, but are psychologically stable. If the brain gets distorted, from the chemical effects of diet, nutrition or training, a mental injury may result. The problem is not uncommon in the athletic community.

Robert was in his third year of shear athletic greatness. His training never felt better, and in a race, he was nearly unbeatable. Always full of energy, and without injury, Robert was climbing the ladder to national success.

But in recent months, Robert has gotten more depressed. And now, his anxiety is more evident as is his dread of competition. He is not only losing his desire to train, but his personal life is being affected as well.

While Robert is not this athlete's real name, his mental injury is authentic.

There are several ways the brain can be injured in the absence of disease. A functional imbalance in the brain's chemistry – a subtle yet noticeable change in certain substances called neurotransmitters – can modify the way we think, feel and act. Fortunately, with few exceptions, these problems are reversible. And more importantly, preventable.

These brain imbalances may be caused by a mismatched diet, a lack or excess of certain nutrients or the end result of overtraining. Let's look at what may have happened to Robert in the months before his mental injury. But first, a quick look at how physical our mental state can be.

Normally, when we think a thought or perceive a sensation from the outside world, it's the result of major chemical reactions in our brain. Billions of messages are sent throughout the brain and body on a regular basis because of chemicals called neurotransmitters.

Different neurotransmitters in our brain make us feel certain ways: high, low, sleepy, awake, happy, sad. Sometimes the brain may have too many of one type of chemical or not enough of another. As a result, we may feel too high or low: agitated or depressed.

Most of the 35 or more neurotransmitters are made from amino acids derived from dietary protein and often influenced by the amount of dietary carbohydrates via the hormone insulin. Two important neurotransmitters are serotonin and norepinephrine.

Serotonin is produced with the help of the amino acid tryptophan, and requires the hormone insulin. This neurotransmitter has a calming, sedating or depressing effect in the brain. A high carbohydrate meal, such as pasta or oatmeal, or eating sweets, results in more serotonin production. So, the individual who is overactive may benefit from a high carbohydrate meal, but those who are a bit low to start may get worse, even to the point of depression. Sweets are traditionally thought of as providing energy, but in actuality they are sedating. (Sometimes, sweets may give the feeling of a pick-up but that is very short lived.) In Robert's case, the over-production of serotonin – a common problem even in athletes – helped establish his mental injury.

Norepinephrine is produced with the help of the amino acid tyrosine, if little of no insulin is present. A high protein meal with little or no carbohydrates will provide the brain with increased norepinephrine levels. This neurotransmitter has a stimulating effect on the brain. The person who needs a pick-up or is depressed could often benefit from more of this brain chemical.

An imbalance in serotonin and norepinephrine – with a shift toward the former – may produce depression. Perhaps Robert was eating too many sweets and other carbohydrates, which made him more depressed. Let's look at the therapeutic options available to him.

Certain drugs are sometimes recommended for patients with chemical imbalances because they can manipulate brain chemistry in the hopes of creating a balance of neurotransmitters. The depressed athlete may be given medication to enhance or block certain neurotransmitters. Prozac, elavil and tofranil are examples of antidepressants which affect the balance of serotonin and norepinephrine, thereby changing the way we feel. (Tranquilizers, such as valium and ativan, function other ways through different neurotransmitters.)

Fortunately, most people do not need medication. But if you are over-active or depressed, you may benefit by simply altering your diet to modify your brain chemistry in the most appropriate way. In Robert's case, decreasing the amount of sugar and other carbohydrates in his diet, and increasing protein foods may be of great value.

If the diet can affect the mental state, then clearly certain nutritional supplements can do the same. That's because specific vitamins and minerals – along with the appropriate amino acid precursors – are required for the brain to make both serotonin and norepinephrine. Some of the more common ones include Vitamin B-6, folic acid, niacin, iron and Vitamin C. But more important are the amino acids tryptophan and tyrosine. All these nutrients – except for tryptophan – are available over-the-counter. (Tryptophan was banned by the FDA a few years ago due to contaminated sources which made some people ill.) The bottom line: Taking too many serotonin precursor nutrients, especially when combined with a high carbohydrate diet, may contribute to a mental injury.

Robert's training may also have contributed to his mental injury. Especially if he was overtrained which results in a stress on his nervous system and emotional instability.

Overtraining frequently is preceded by too much anaerobic work. While we're familiar with the relationship between lactic acid and anaerobic exercise, most have not heard of its effect on the mental state. For a long time, scientists have known that increased lactic acid – more specifically, lactate – in the body may provoke depression, anxiety and phobias.

This occurs due to an over-stimulation of the adrenal glands (and occurs with the release of endorphins) and an over-excitation of the nervous system – the same pattern seen in overtraining. It has even been shown that infusion of lactate into relatively normal subjects produces anxiety, depression and panic.

Given this, perhaps Robert produced too much lactic acid – from training or racing.

Fortunately, Robert can get himself out of his crisis. While it's not impossible for him to do it alone, more than likely he'll find it easier if he gets help: from a friend, family member or professional. Whatever the case, it's important to look at the whole picture.

The big picture includes, what happened at the onset. Was Robert training beyond his ability? Was he racing too much, or eating wrong? More often it's a combination of actions. Sitting down and assessing each aspect of his life is a good first step for Robert. Being objective is the hard part – and that's where other's are helpful. Accepting that there really is a problem may also be a difficult hill to climb.

Making the appropriate changes, whatever they may be, can often result in a speedy remedy. within a couple of weeks – or sooner – Robert can be feeling better, and portray noticeable changes to others around him.

Chapter 18

Mending Your Own Injury

"The doctor who treats himself has a fool for a patient." I recall that comment from my later years in school. The same holds true for the athlete. It's very difficult to be as objective with your own ills as someone else can be.

But for years, I've also encountered countless athletes who sought care for simple injuries but could not be helped. There are many good doctors and therapists around. But unfortunately, there are many more incompetent ones.

When you're injured, or when you feel something is heading that way, the ideal scenario is to seek out the help of a professional. This may be in the form of a doctor, massage therapist, physical therapist, etc. As long as your problem is corrected – I should say the cause of your problem – with no side effects, it doesn't matter what methods are used.

Often I am asked, "what can I do for my _____." You fill in the blank – ilio tibial band syndrome, knee problem, back pain, etc. The list is long.

Physical injuries are an epidemic in the athletic population. One reason is overtraining. By far the best way to solve this chronic problem is to prevent injuries. But that doesn't help the thousands who are right now afflicted with some injury.

Here's the first step; don't treat the name. There's no cook book cure for ilio tibial band syndrome or low back pain. The reality is that everyone's ITB problem is different. So from the start, let's forget about the name – it has hardly any worthy meaning.

Instead, lets find out what the problem is, or is not. And what you can do to help your body correct its own problems. After all, that's what it supposed to do.

Generally speaking, most injuries are not serious. However, if they are not corrected and continue to prevent you from training, they may end your athletic career.

What I want to say is that most injuries are functional rather than pathological. Functional problems are likened to your car not starting – there's some relatively minor problem which is easily corrected by the right mechanic; if you can find one.

A pathological problem is one where you need a new engine, or a new car – the problem is often very serious. A broken bone, a tumor, or an injury that can only be corrected by a surgical procedure are usually more serious problems. In general, these conditions require more radical care rather than conservative treatment. Fortunately, pathological problems in endurance athletes are not common. Unfortunately, many athletes and professionals use words which describe pathological problems when the injury is simply functional.

Functional problems are often soft tissue injuries – from simple muscle imbalances to minor ligament or tendon strain or sprain. As opposed to pathological injuries, functional problems are usually correctable with more conservative measures, and quite often by the person who has them. So what can you do to help correct your own injury? Here are some general suggestions that have been proved successful over time. Don't underestimate the simplicity of these items; most injuries have simple remedies.

1. Find an activity that does not aggravate the problem, and do it. One of the worse problems with the injured athlete is inactivity. This lack of training becomes an aggravating factor. Walking is a great remedy if it doesn't hurt. Running in a pool is also good. Four feet of water will provide some but not too much gravity stress. Stationary equipment sometimes works well. Try to spend the same amount of time doing these activities (or combinations) as you would your normal workout.

If you have pain as part of your injury picture, let it guide you. The best rule to follow regarding pain; if it improves as your workout progresses, that's generally a good sign. If the pain isn't exacerbated following the activity, that's even better. But if the pain gets worse with your activity, stop. Either try another activity or wait a couple of days and try to workout again, following the rules below.

2. Make sure you warm up properly with all your activities. Both warm up and cool down has a therapeutic type effect on your whole body – from muscles to metabolism. In many cases, lengthening your warm up and cool down time can also greatly help.

3. Avoid stretching. Many injuries are the result of over-stretched muscles, with tightness developing as a secondary problem.

4. Keep all your workouts strictly aerobic until your injury heals. Be even more conservative with your maximum aerobic heart rate. Avoid all weight lifting, anaerobic intervals and other hard workouts.

5. Take a good look at your shoes, whether your problem is running related or not (even the shoes you wear through the day may cause problems). Replace them if there's excessive wear or weakened supports.

6. Occasionally, if an athlete can not get to my clinic, I may recommend they take three days off as a therapy. Most often, this approach is done before an injury has become extreme, in its early stages. This give the body a chance to recover and possibly correct its own problems. Resumption of training should be cautious for about a week to make sure the problem does not recur.

The most important aspect of an injury is that it should teach you something about your training, racing or equipment. Once you've learned that, you'll become more immune to injuries, and more efficient with training and racing.

Chapter 19

Your Most Important Endurance Muscle: The Diaphragm

Of all the vital muscles necessary for optimal endurance, perhaps the most important one is the diaphragm. This large flat muscle allows us to breathe; it pulls in oxygenated air and expels unwanted carbon dioxide, a more important item to remove than taking in oxygen.

In well trained endurance athletes, the breathing mechanism may be the weak link in good performance. In this case, less air enters the lungs and the blood does not receive the proper amount of oxygen necessary to feed the rest of the body.

The diaphragm is also directly associated with other muscles. Particularly the psoas major muscle, your most important hip flexor, which has attachments to the diaphragm. Muscles between the ribs, the intercostals, and some of the neck muscles are also important for breathing. During hard activity, 15% of the oxygen consumed is used by the breathing muscles. Even at rest, up to 12% of the oxygen consumption is used for respiration.

An important relationship exists between the diaphragm and the abdominal muscles. Our culture has produced an attitude that makes us overly anxious about our abdominal muscles. Most people think a flat, hard belly is ideal. And many athletes achieve this. But if the abdominal muscles are too tight, it will inhibit the function of the diaphragm, adversely effecting our oxygen intake and carbon dioxide removal. This is a common problem in endurance athletes, and usually results from strengthening techniques using sit-up, crunches and abdominal machines. Endurance athletes don't want the high powered steel-like abdominals like we see in body builders. What's more important is the power of the diaphragm.

One of the problems with disturbing the delicate balance between the diaphragm and the abdominal muscles is it often changes the way you breathe. Here is an example of the normal breathing mechanism:

1. During inhalation, the abdominal muscles relax and are gently pushed out, allowing the diaphragm muscle to contract and lower. There is also a simultaneous but slight extension of the spine.

2. Exhalation involves the contracting, or pulling in of the abdominal muscles, with slight flexion of the spine.

3. The chest should move very little during normal breathing, and should expand only during more forced inhalation, and only after the abdominals have relaxed (i.e., are pushed out).

When training and racing, additional expansion of the lungs is necessary. In this case the chest expands on inhalation, but only after abdominal relaxation and diaphragm contraction.

This sounds easy enough, but many athletes breathe just the opposite way: they pull their abdomen in when inhaling and expand their chest. As a result, less air and oxygen is taken into the lungs, with less carbon dioxide removed. This can be a cumulative stress on the entire system over time, especially during racing.

If you're breathing incorrectly, you must first re-learn the normal mechanism. Stand with one hand on the mid to lower abdomen, and one hand on the lower spine, and slowly practice breathing in and out. Think of the area where your hands are as a vessel, which you are attempting to fill with air.

Another method of training the diaphragm muscle is the straw exercise. This helps improve the power of the muscle, and involves breathing deeply, and slowly, in and out of a straw for one to two minutes. Work up to several sets of two minutes each three times a week for eight to 10 weeks. This may be very difficult at first for someone with a weak diaphragm, but soon you will have no trouble.

There are also some simple tests you or a professional can perform to measure diaphragm function.

The Vital Capacity is a good test for measuring lung capacity and general diaphragm function. Vital capacity is related to physiological age: the lower the vital capacity, the older you are physiologically, and vice versa.

A simple test you can do yourself is to measure Breath-Holding Time. This measures the general capacity of the diaphragm, and lung volume. Take a deep breath and see how long you can hold it. Anyone in good health should be able to hold the breath for at least 50 to 60 seconds.

Another test related to the diaphragm is Snider's Test, which measures the strength of the diaphragm using the power in the breath. Hold a small lit match six inches away from your mouth. With your mouth wide open, try to blow the match out. You should be able to do so easily.

Chapter 20

Training Shoes

All shoe companies make good shoes; your job is to find the right ones for your feet.

Modern runners have a choice to make when working out on their feet. It's the decision to wear shoes or train barefoot. Of course almost all choose to wear shoes. But there's a price to pay; wearing running shoes costs not only in energy, but in the real possibility of excess biomechanical stress leading to injury. Not to mention to price tag.

A little bit of weight added to your feet produces large negative effects in the economy of locomotion. For example, for every three ounces of running shoe weight, there is a 1% increase in oxygen uptake required.

But the problem goes beyond that. Did you also know that the support systems in almost all shoes can weaken your ankles? And the soft, cushioned shoes can potentially lead to injury? And, the thicker the sole the more unstable your foot becomes.

Scientific studies strongly suggests that the protective features put in by shoe companies, including shock absorption and motion control actually increase the likelihood of injury.

Here are some of the reasons.

The soles of our feet have millions of nerve endings which sense the pounding and stress of running. Your brain and body work together to adapt to this stress by constantly adjusting your gait during running. This normal protective mechanism keeps us from being injured. When we cover our foot with a shoe, we interfere with this adaptive mechanism. The result is a diminished ability by the foot to adapt, with potential damage to the ligaments, fascia, cartilage or bone in not only the foot, but the leg, thigh, pelvis, low back or many other area.

Ideally, barefoot is best because there is no interference with the nerves that sense our contacts with the ground. Unfortunately, it's not as practical as it once was.

An important fact to remember is this: The impact which results from training occurs whether a shoe is worn or not.

Many shoe support systems, including orthotics, can interfere with the normal functioning of the medial arch. I will only on rare occasions recommend orthotics, and only for a short time while the cause of the problem is corrected.

Sorbothane is a commonly used material in running shoes. While tests on machines demonstrate its great energy absorbing abilities, a study on humans shows that insoles made of this material actually increase leg stress by 26%. Another study showed an increase in foot and leg injuries.

In a study of 5,000 runners, those using more expensive running shoes (those with more shock absorbing materials) had a higher incidence of injury. So it seems there is less chance of getting a running injury in less expensive shoes.

Shoes with more cushioning are also likely to produce excessive pronation, especially with the added soft midsole material.

Heel height can also increase pronation, especially in shoes with heels that are thicker than about one inch.

But beware; the muscles of your foot and leg, especially the calf muscles, have adapted to the thickness of your shoe. If you suddenly change your shoe style, your muscles may have to re-adjust their length. This may take a couple of weeks, during which you may experience some calf discomfort.

Another problem with higher heels is that it forces you to run too far back on the shoe rather than striking the ground farther forward. This exaggerated heel-toe gait is a walking style and not good or efficient for running.

So now what do you wear?

Basically all the shoe companies make some good running shoes. Try the flat racer/trainer types. In some cases, a racing shoe works well for daily training.

If you're concerned about the steep price of today's shoes, consider other sources. I've been training in a pair of running shoes I get in Walmart or K-Mart for under ten dollars.

Chapter 21

The Short Shoe Syndrome

Like overtraining, wearing shoes that don't match the body's needs have become common place. For a significant number of athletes, their training shoes are too small. Wearing shoes that are too small can cause pain or dysfunction in the ankle, leg, knee, hip, low back, and at times even in the cervical spine or temporal mandibular jaw joint.

A study done in my clinic over an 18 month period found 52% of the new athletic patients were training in shoes too small. Once the problem was diagnosed, these patients usually required a change from one-half to 1½ sizes larger.

Case History
Jim was the classic patient who saw eight different doctors for his problems. Because his symptoms were in both knees, most of the therapeutic attention was directed there. Although his history was unremarkable when first visiting me, his shoes told the story. Jim's right shoe had an area where the large toenail had worn through. Upon measuring his foot, it was found his shoes were a whole size too small. "I thought they should be snug," he said. "My bike shoes are even smaller." After buying larger shoes, Jim was able to exercise without pain for the first time in 2½ years.

Why Foot Size Changes
You might think that the size of your feet is set by age 20, but this isn't true. Normal size changes, as a result of weight gain or loss, gait problems, muscular imbalance and pregnancy, occur regardless of age. The increase is due to the relaxation or elongation of the ligaments and tendons, followed by an expansion of the bones in the foot. Generally, the more weight bearing type training, such as running, the greater the likelihood that your feet will become larger after the age of 20. Even if you spend all day at your job standing on your feet, your required shoes size can change.

Some athletes, having bought larger shoes after the initial diagnosis, experienced continued enlargement of their feet, eventually ending with a total difference of up to 2½ sizes!

First Metatarsal Jam

Training in a shoe that's too small – too short a length – results in a slow jamming of the toes, characteristically causing a backward subluxation of the first metatarsal joint. This creates a mechanical instability in the foot which, if left uncorrected, can lead to other foot and ankle problems such as hammer toes and bunions. In time, the toes become spring-like; when a small shoe is slipped on, the toes spring in, and the tightness of the shoe is not obvious. The first metatarsal joint, however, is not as flexible as the joints of other toes, and therefore takes most of the abuse.

Diagnosing the Problem

Due to the slow onset of this common problem, the first metatarsal jam is often asymptomatic; if you have it you usually don't complain of pain in that first toe joint.

But visual examination of your feet will reveal trauma, or micro-trauma (long lasting mild stress) to the front of the foot. This often includes dis-coloration of the nail bed (black toenail), blistering or callousing of the toes, or swelling of the first metatarsal joint (the ball of the foot). In more extreme cases, inspection of your shoe will reveal wear and tear, inside and out, as a result of the nail or front of the toe trying to push out of the shoe.

Take out and study the insert in your shoe. Look at the wear pattern (the indentation made from the toes) on this insert, and see if the areas com-pressed by the toes are not completely on the insert. A foot that overlaps the top of the insert obviously is in the wrong size shoe.

The importance of proper fitting shoes cannot be overemphasized. Below are tips on finding an ideal fitting shoe:

1. Measure your foot. After a certain age, people often don't have their feet measured when buying new shoes, since they don't realize their size could have changed. As a result, the same shoe size is worn for years, or even decades.

Have both feet measured by a competent shoe store salesperson, being sure they are measured in a standing position on a hard floor. It may be necessary to have your feet measured two or even three times during the day, due to normal size fluctuations. (Of course, any meaningful daily size fluctuations must be differentiated from serious health problems, such as swelling and certain pathological changes.) Compare the actual size of the foot with the shoe size (measured) currently being worn.

2. Spend adequate time trying on shoes in the store. Find a hard surface rather than the thick soft carpet found in many shoe stores, where almost any shoe will feel good. If there is no sturdy floor to walk on, ask if you can walk outside. (If you can't, shop elsewhere). Try on the size you normally wear. Even if that feels fine, try on a half size larger. If that one feels the same (or even better), try on another half size larger. Continue trying on larger half sizes until you find the shoes that are obviously too large. Then go back to the previous half-size and usually that's the best one. You may need to try different widths to get a perfect fit, which is what you should strive for. Don't let anyone say that you will have to break them in before they feel good. Even though you may develop the reputation of being a nuisance at your shoe store, your body will benefit. It would also be worth educating the salespeople if they are unaware of these types of problems.

3. For those people who have a significant difference of more than a half size between their two feet, it may be best to wear two different sized shoes. If this is the case with you, write the shoe company whose shoes you like, and explain your situation, they may help. If the difference between the two feet is less than a half size, fit the larger foot.

4. When it comes to training shoes, more women fit and function better in men's shoes than in women's. Rule #1 though, is that the shoe must fit properly. Some women don't fit into men's shoes, and some stores don't carry men's shoes in sizes that are small enough for some women.

5. You may not find the right shoe in the first store you go to. Most outlets carry only a few of the many shoes in the marketplace. Often, shoes from mail order outlets cost less. But be prepared for the hassle of shipping back those that don't quite fit right.

6. Remember, the manufacturer makes new shoes based on trends of style, color and fancy gimmicks used to market the shoe. That is why many shoes come and go in the market so frequently. So if you finally find the shoe that works great for you, buy several pairs. Just be sure to try them all on, since the same shoe style may vary in size.

Chapter 22

Women & Endurance: Naturally Superior?

For decades – more accurately, centuries – women have been deceived, cheated and denied their right to use their natural power of endurance. Assorted reasons have not only been given, but were the social norms as to why the female of the human species should not, and could not, be interested in or preoccupied by sports, especially the endurance variety.

Yes, we have most women's sports in most schools, but still there are the holdouts – in cycling, the Tour de France is without women. Most professional sports are comprised of all men. Until the 1960s, females were prohibited from running races longer than 800-meters. They were also barred from official participation from the marathon until the 1970s, with the women's Olympic Marathon debut coming as late as 1984. In that race, Joan Benoit's 2:24 would have won 11 of the previous 20 men's Olympic marathons.

Today, the female endurance athlete has arrived, but her acceptance has not really been as complete a success as has the men she races against. At least yet.

Fortunately, women have gained more equality than in many other sports. But in this endurance world, women still have one last step to attain; that of outperforming her male counterpart.

What is generally missed is the fact that women in the endurance field can be equal to or excel over men. It has led scientists to ask if the difference between male and female performance is all biological, or if there is a major social impediment, preventing women from achieving their full endurance potential.

The differences in men and women are obvious; the structural, chemical and mental aspects empower each to function as efficiently as nature intended. But in the natural evolution of the human species, one aspect that was essential to survival was endurance. And men and women developed it equally.

When the topic of the female athlete is brought up, the discussion usually reverts to the power comparisons between male and female, menstrual problems, osteoporosis, eating disorders and other "special" concerns for female athletes. Even the danger of women training alone becomes a main issue unique to women. While all these concerns are important, they should not be the primary focus. Nor should their difference be distorted.

Body composition of females is nearly identical to males for the first dozen or so years of life. For example, fat-free body mass averages are the same until about the age of 13. At this time, different hormonal changes between the sexes produce the contrasts we are all familiar with. In the case of the female at puberty, the pituitary hormones trigger the ovaries to develop and produce estrogen. This hormone, among other actions, increases stored fat, primarily necessary for pregnancy and lactation.

In the male at puberty, the same pituitary hormone results in testosterone production. This hormone provides for a larger body frame and muscle mass. But women produce some testosterone as well, and men manufacture some estrogen.

It is the consequences of these hormonal events that comparisons are made between men and women athletes. In addition, other differences are measurable, especially those related to the responses to training.

For example, because of the larger quantity of muscle, men tend to be stronger in power. Unfortunately, this leads some to infer that women are the "weaker" sex. (Ashley Montague's *Natural Superiority of Women* looks at this issue in a broader, more natural view.) However, when other factors are considered (such as comparing absolute strength to free-fat mass), the differences are much less significant or there are none at all. Women can improve strength dramatically, but without the major increase in muscle mass seen in men. (The decreased muscle mass in women is compensated for by improved neurological function.)

Endurance sports are not true power events, where muscle bulk is key. If that were the case, just lifting weights would provide the advantage, and almost all men would cross the finish line before even the first women. But the primary "power" in endurance events comes from aerobic function.

Endurance capacity is often measured using VO_2 max. Females reach their peak VO_2 max in early teens where males reach theirs around age 20, and maintain higher levels than women. But the average woman athlete has a VO_2 max that's only 8-12% lower than the average man. Women are also capable of experiencing the same relative increase in VO_2 max as men.

But endurance events are not won by the athlete with the highest VO2 max. Nor are these races all out sprints or power events. So the submaximal oxygen consumption may be of greater importance – not only in the race itself but in the training required. And when submaximal VO2 is compared, little if any difference is found between men and women.

Studies done on middle and long-distance runners show that women's peak lactate values are significantly lower – 45% less – than men's. And, when expressed in relative terms, anaerobic threshold values are similar in men and women.

Women possess a greater capacity than men to burn fat. Improving their metabolism through training and diet to burn more fat may give them the edge since fat burning is a key in endurance events. Unfortunately, too many women still adhere to a low fat diet, it may contribute to ill health, with amenorrhea as a common end result.

In addition to burning more fat, trained women seem to have lower stress (indicated by lower epinephrine levels) and less muscle glycogen depletion during endurance training.

How does all this translate into real life issues of racing? Can a finely tuned woman beat an equally finely tuned man in an Ironman? If so, will they then change the name to Ironwoman? We may have to wait for the answers, but probably not too long.

Changing tradition and social customs takes time. Only recently (since the '70s) have some young girls developed with as much physical activity as their boy counterparts. And this is still not the norm. Girls are just now beginning to be trained as hard as boys. Once that happened, their performances improved dramatically and should continue to do so.

If recent history is an indication, we may be seeing more women outperforming more men. In the 400-meter freestyle, the winning time for the women in the 1924 Olympic Games was 16% slower than the men. In 1948, this difference shrunk to 11.6%, and in 1984 diminished to only 6.9%. And the men's world record time for the 800-meter freestyle set in 1972, was bettered by a women just 7 years later. Other sports follow this pattern of closing the gap in performance.

The 1995 second place finisher at the Leadville 100-mile running race was Ann Trason. Her time was eighteen hours:40 minutes – only 6 minutes behind the leader! Paula Newby-Fraser's sub 9-hour Ironman performances are only bested by a very small number of men. And the record for swimming the English Channel is held by a women at 7 hours:40 minutes. The best men's time is 32 minutes slower at 8 hours:12 minutes.

Are there really any differences in training and dietary needs for women compared to men, as indicated by advertisers and tradition?. In my experience, no. My approach is based on individualization, and I don't use different training methods because the athlete is female. In laboratory measurements, I don't observe increased needs for iron in women as compared to men (iron is also lost in sweat). The same is true for calcium, or protein, or any nutrient. This as long as the diet is personalized and effective.

It is my feeling that in the coming years women endurance athletes will improve at a faster rate than will men. More women will break into the top 10 or 20 at races of all levels. And women will start competing for the top spots in the big races.

Chapter 23

If Einstein Were Your Coach

Whether you're just beginning your endurance career or training for a double Ironman, Albert Einstein would say the key to an effective program is taking charge of the time element.

Einstein said, "Time is relative." He postulated that a spacecraft leaving earth and traveling near the speed of light for 20 years would return to earth with a different record of time elapsed than that on earth. Comparing two identical clocks, one on the spacecraft and one on earth, the spacecraft clock may show 10 years had elapsed, but the clock on earth would show 20 years had passed. Moreover, the passengers on the spacecraft would have aged only 10 years while those on earth had aged 20 years in that same time. This view of two clocks providing us with different times of the same event can be useful in our training for endurance.

We all know the human body can sense and react to time differently, given the same situation. A successful race seems to pass more quickly than one in which you are struggling. "Time is not a constant thing by any means," says Olympic marathoner Lorraine Moller of New Zealand. "When you're in a good race, everything comes together. Time flies when you're having fun."

Time can be experienced as a non-flowing, isolated part of any performance; the event does not take place as most see it, but differently. This view of time is most evident when we're falling in love, meditating or in a trance. As Larry Dossey, M.D., states in his book *Space, Time, and Medicine*, "These experiences suggest that an alternative to the ordinary means of experiencing time lies within all of us." In our fast-paced society, we always seem to run out of time. This, among other things, creates stress.

If you're rushing through your workouts, not "taking the time" to enjoy them, this stress may eventually have a negative influence on your entire health and fitness.

Tim is a common example of another kind of time problem. The remedy is something Albert Einstein could provide.

Case History

> *Tim had been running regularly for five years, and at age 37 was training for his fourth marathon. He was hoping to break the elusive three-hour barrier, which he had been close to three time previous. His training schedule included the traditional "long" Sunday run of two hours, and would soon increase so his "longest" run would be two-and-a-half hours. However, relative to even his "longest" run, how will Tim relate to the time it will take him to run the three-hour marathon? In other words, for Tim, two hours was long, two-and-a-half hours longest...was three hours reasonable? Tim needed to modify his approach or he'd fail to attain his goal, as so many do in events that have significant time factors. He had to relate both psychologically and physiologically to three hours as short.*

Einstein was able to understand and relate to complex issues, but how could he help Tim, or anyone else in their relatively simple quests? Using our earlier notion that an event can be viewed through two clocks will help anyone to control time more effectively.

"A lot of coping with time," Lorraine Moller says, "is just learning to relax." You might try relaxing in front of a clock with a large second hand that clicks off the seconds. Stare at it. Notice that some seconds seem longer, or shorter, than others. And if you "play" a little, you may find you can "hold" the second hand in one place for, what would seem to be several seconds.

Tim also had a problem with two clocks. He wanted his marathon clock to read less time than the observed time; he wanted the race to feel more like an hour. One of Tim's downfalls was that he was using his longest run to train for an event that would take more time than the training run itself. In other words, the marathon was even longer than his longest run. Tim had to experience a workout of more than three hours, without overtraining, so the marathon would be relatively shorter. He also had to learn how to manipulate time at will.

Walking was one remedy for both of these time problems. By adding more time to his long run, by walking the first and the last half hour, Tim could increase the total time of his long training session without risking overtraining. Walking also relaxed him in a way running never did.

After two or three of these workouts, Tim learned how easy it was to manipulate time. His total workout of 3.5 hours (a half-hour walk, 2.5 hour run, and a half-hour walk), enabled him to either make the time go faster, or, because he didn't want the now enjoyable workout to end, go slower. These workouts would re-orient Tim, making the marathon shorter, relative to the long workout. On marathon day, he would be able to make the marathon go by quickly.

This is just what happened, since Tim ran his race in 2 hours and 48 minutes, saying afterwards, "It felt like an easy long run."

These time tactics helped Stu Mittleman attain his world record in the 1,000-Mile Run. This event required a modification of the relationship of time to enable Stu to cope with the 1,000 one-mile laps. Averaging approximately 86 miles a day, Stu successfully manipulated time so that the 11-plus days were psychologically and physiologically less than 11 days. "By the fifth day," Stu recalls, "if you'd ask me how many days went by, I'd say two."

We used these same time games to train Paul Fendler who, in his first-ever ultra-marathon distance, became the Metropolitan Athletic Congress 50-Mile Champion in 1987. "All of a sudden, in the beginning of the race, time ceased to be an existing factor," Fendler recalls, "and it was the walk/run workouts that taught me how to control time."

Einstein thought in holistic terms, and believed that the universe doesn't contain random activity. This certainly includes the organization of the human body and the influence of many factors which affect our training and racing. The aspect of time is merely one of those factors.

Chapter 24

The Experimental Use of Mild Hyperbaric Chambers

Treating and training athletes always involves some aspect of experimentation. That may include diet, nutrition, training or techniques and other therapies that pose no danger to the athlete. For more than a decade, I have used a mild hyperbaric chamber with many athletes and have found it to be of great benefits as a therapeutic instrument. The improvements in recovery and race preparedness seem to be derived from the increase in oxygen uptake, even though no added oxygen is used in the hyperbaric chamber.

In contrast to high altitude environments, where oxygen uptake is diminished, high pressure environments produce an increased oxygen uptake. This condition can occur at low altitude, inside a hyperbaric chamber, and to a lesser degree, during high pressure weather systems.

Traditionally, hyperbaric chambers are generally used for first-aid purposes. The most common applications include treatment of mountain climbers, underwater divers and pilots for decompression sickness, resulting from too rapid or extreme a change in pressure exerted on the body. In recent years, cardiac patients, burn victims and some people with chronic infections, including AIDS, have also been treated in hyperbaric chambers. Many of these chambers are very high pressure devices, sometimes referred to as "Iron lungs" where additional oxygen is also used.

In the mid 1980s, Dr. Igor Gamow of Boulder, Colorado, invented a portable, mild hyperbaric chamber for first aid use in mountain climbers. Having an interest in altitude and pressure relationships in health and fitness, I decided to try this device with a few athletes.

This mild hyperbaric chamber, called the Gamow Bag, is a 17-cubic foot non-permeable nylon cylinder-shaped "bag" with an air-tight zipper. It is inflated with an oil-free medical compressor, and the environment is regulated through pressure-controlled vents. A continuous flow of incoming and outgoing air prevents carbon dioxide build-up.

The higher pressure in the chamber mimics the pressure of lower altitudes. For example, if you used this mild hyperbaric chamber in Boulder, Colorado, (altitude 5,000 feet) the pressure inside the chamber would increase and mimic near sea level conditions. The higher you ascend in altitude, the lower the pressure, with lower altitudes creating higher pressures. The higher the pressure (low altitudes) the higher the oxygen uptake. For example, at sea level, you will take up more oxygen from the air than in Colorado, which is higher in altitude.

How significant is this added oxygen uptake? Descending from 1,763 meters to sea level, an increased pressure of only 53 mm Hg, will increase oxygen uptake by over 11%. A descent of 3,000 meters, increases the total oxygen uptake by over 17%! This increase is likened to that obtained through many months or even years of training.

I have used the Gamow Bag as a therapy to speed recovery from training, prepare an athlete for racing, and as adjunctive therapeutic agent in the treatment of many athletic problems. Empirically, the hyperbaric chamber also seems to benefit those having difficulty losing body fat.

More research is needed in this field to find out what changes take place and what protocol is most useful for which types of training and health conditions. In 1990, the U.S. Olympic Committee completed a pilot study using the Gamow Bag on elite runners. The research staff included Peter Van Handle, PhD, and concluded that "exposure to a hyperbaric environment may improve maximal work capacity."

To date, I have observed no negative effects as a result of the use of mild hyperbaric chambers. However, continued exposure to the hyperbaric environment, hence increased oxygen uptake, may produce nutritional deficiencies if subjects are not eating properly. An identical state may occur in athletes who have trained regularly for many months on a poor diet. Eventually, the need for certain nutrients increases as oxygen uptake increases due to training. This problem is not created by the hyperbaric chamber, but becomes evident sooner than it would have without use of the chamber.

Hyperbaria and Hyperoxia
Increasing the pressure of ambient air as a means of increasing oxygen uptake is referred to as hyperbaria. This is not the same as increasing the total oxygen content of air, such as breathing pure oxygen, which is called hyperoxia. It has been argued that no difference exists between hyperbaria and the result of breathing pure oxygen without hyperbaria. But many experts agree that hyperbaria (increased pressure) and hyperoxia (increased oxygen) are not the same. One important difference is in the

oxygen and carbon dioxide levels of the blood flow to the brain. Hyperoxia actually lowers blood flow to the brain. In general, breathing high concentrations of oxygen can even lower general arterial oxygen levels, increase free radicals and even create an oxygen toxicity.

Mild hyperbaric chambers are now readily available. Hyperbaric Technologies, Inc. (Amsterdam, NY 800-382-2491) is marketing the original "bag" chamber, which can be packed up in a small suitcase for travel.

The future of sports training will certainly include the use of mild hyperbaric equipment.

Chapter 25

A Note About Nutrition & Diet

A book on training provides only one aspect of sport. Others include such topics as psychology, aerodynamics, nutrition and diet.

In the case of nutrition and diet, it's not possible to cover that vast topic in one chapter. Nor will I try to do that. But there are a few point I would like to make on the subject, with the probability that an entire book will be forthcoming.

Most cells of the body have a certain lifespan. For example, our red blood cells live about four months. When they die, some of their parts are recycled, but, for the most part, new materials are formulated to create a whole new red blood cell.

An important question is, where does the body get these new materials? The answer is simple: from the macro and micronutrients in your diet.

The macronutrients include the three main building blocks of our physiology; carbohydrates, proteins and fats. The micronutrients are the vitamins, minerals and other elements necessary to regulate macronutrient activity. All these substances provide us with energy, and new materials to make new cells.

Essentially, the athlete you are this year is different than who you were last year. This is true not only on a biological level – where most of the cells replace themselves – but more so on a molecular level. In this latter case, molecules replace themselves billions at a time with each breath we take in.

If you want to build a better athlete beginning right now, the quality of the food you consume must be the best you can get; the freshest, least processed, and most natural available.

The phrase, "you are what you eat" can be applied to endurance athletes just as well as anyone else. Consider the very brief introduction to macronutrients given below.

Our energy, whether at rest or during running, comes from the macronutrients in our diet – carbohydrates, fats and proteins. The amount of each we eat may help or hinder our performance, depending on our specific requirements. And everyone is uniquely different. Finding your needs should be a priority if you want to improve your overall health and running fitness.

Significant amounts of our energy can come from fats. The more fat we burn, the less we'll store, and the more endurance we'll develop. But for many runners, that four-letter word – fats – has a negative tone. Perhaps it's time to change our tune.

We have enough stored energy from carbohydrates to get us 20 miles into a marathon. If not for fat, it would be impossible to finish the last 10K. And protein can give us an energy bonus of 10%. One of the keys to getting our food to work right is diet. Let's look at each of the macronutrients and how they could play a role in improving your running.

The average person has enough stored fat to power them through dozens of marathons. This untapped power and endurance source is available, if our body is programmed to use it. But the "low fat trend" has only helped turn off our fat burning efforts, forcing us to use more carbohydrates and less fats in our running. Eating some fat can assist your body in this effort.

Not just any fats, but "good" fats. In the coming years you'll be hearing more about the merits of fats. Besides giving us energy, they help fight stress and inflammation, assist our immune system, offer protection from injury and help get calcium into our bones.

The good fats are the ones nature has provided: vegetable oils, nuts, butter, cream, eggs, etc. But, we want to be sure we eat more vegetable and other non-animal fats, than saturated animal fats – about twice as much. And remember, butter, eggs and even meats contain some of the same fats found in olive and canola oil.

Fats are an essential part of a good diet. No scientist can deny that. We now know that diets that are very low in fat can contribute to heart disease. And the fats found in olive oil helps prevent breast cancer. For runners, fats also help performance.

A diet that's about 25-30% fat is a reasonable amount when viewing macronutrient intake in this new light. For some athletes, 35% or more is necessary for their individual needs. World champion ultramarathoner Stu Mittleman consumes this percentage – or more – when training for his races.

Fats to avoid include the over-cooked ones, especially when fried, and hydrogenated fats found in many products (just read the labels). The most common hydrogenated product is margarine. (It's not nice to fool mother nature.) Margarine can make your cholesterol picture much worse because it acts even worse than a saturated fat.

But we can't burn fats without carbohydrates. Balance is the key; too much or too little fat or carbohydrate can create problems. In my experience, many people are avoiding too much fat and eating too many carbs.

Excess carbohydrates, especially refined ones like white pasta and sugar, can turn off our ability to burn fats.

Consuming carbohydrates stimulates the release of the hormone insulin, which causes a drop in blood sugar. Insulin sends this blood sugar to the cells and increases glycogen storage; essentially it compels your body to use more carbohydrates as fuel. More importantly, insulin converts about 40% of your carbohydrates to fat for storage. If you want to use more fats for energy, the insulin response must be moderated. High glycemic foods – such as pasta, cereals, fruit juice and all sugars – results in more insulin being released, more fat stored and less fat burned.

In many people, this scenario produces excess hunger, moodiness, fatigue, headaches, depression, and other blood sugar symptoms. Also, sleepiness after meals and intestinal bloating are common symptoms of excess carbohydrate intake.

If you want to use more fats and improve endurance, consider moderating (ideally, eliminating) the intake of refined sugars, and keeping all other carbohydrate intake to about 35-50% of the diet.

Like fat, protein has also been ignored in recent years. The RDA for protein has been revised at least 10 times since 1943 and continues to be a topic for debate. Many feel todays recommendation – 0.8/kg body weight – is too low, with some experts suggesting amounts three to four times the RDA.

Athletes involved in activities which build muscle and endurance, and are subjected to recurring trauma may need larger protein intakes. Once optimal body size is attained and growth stabilizes, there is still significant and continuous turnover of tissue protein, especially in runners.

The traditional view that higher protein intakes are only required by weight lifters is outdated. Today we know that aerobic endurance training may increase the need for protein even more than anaerobic muscle-building exercise.

Sample meals that are lower in carbohydrate with 30% fat and protein:

8 oz. tomato juice, 2 poached eggs on 2 slices of multi-grain toast (dry), ½ cup low fat cottage cheese.

Chicken salad with mayo on whole wheat bread, a mixed salad (lettuce, onions, carrots), extra virgin olive oil and vinegar.

Broiled fish, ½ cup brown rice, ½ cup 3-bean salad, ½ cup cooked zucchini.

The Athlete's Secret Nutrient
Of all the micro and macronutrients that are important in overall health and fitness, there is one nutrient even more important. This substance is the most inexpensive and most readily available, but is the most deficient of all nutrients in athletes.

What is this powerful dietary nutrient? Water. Most athletes don't get enough of it during rest, training and racing.

In most endurance events, the majority of competitors finish the race dehydrated. Unfortunately, too many of them start the race the same way. In a 2½ hour endurance event, for example, water loss may reduce body water content by up to 10% – despite efforts to drink enough water. This is a significant and dangerous situation which effects both your health and performance.

Of all the nutritional needs, water is the most important. It is the second most important substance second only to oxygen. About 60% or more of a male athletes weight is water, slightly less for females. Normally, about two-thirds of our supply comes from drinking fluids (mostly water) and a third from foods (about 10% is produced by our cells during the conversion of carbohydrates and fats to energy).

Water input must balance water loss, both at rest and during exercise. Water loss occurs from several areas of the body.

Evaporation of water from the skin is important to control body temperature. Even under cool, resting conditions, about 30% of our water loss occurs here. But during endurance activity, sweating increases this amount dramatically – about 300 times the amount lost during rest! The amount is determined in part by the temperature of the air (the higher the temperature the more water loss), and the body size (the larger the person the more water loss).

Water lost in exhaled air is also a significant amount. The air going into and out of our lungs needs to be humidified. Due to the increased breathing rate during exercise and racing, this amount of water loss is increased five to ten times.

Most of the water lost during rest occurs through the kidneys. This water is used to help eliminate waste products from the body. But during exercise, the body attempts to conserve water, and loss through the kidney is very limited – 50 to 70 times less than when at rest. And small but significant water loss (about 5%) is through the intestine at rest. Unless an athlete has diarrhea during an event, there is no water loss from the intestine during exercise or competition.

One of the biggest problems of dehydration – excess water loss – is that it decreases blood volume. Maintaining blood volume is important because of so many vital functions it is associated with:

- Red blood cells carry oxygen to the muscles via blood.

- Nutrients, including glucose, fats and amino acids, are transported in the blood.

- Through the blood, carbon dioxide and other waste products are removed.

- Hormones that regulate muscular activity during exercise (and aid in recovery) are carried by the blood.

- The blood neutralizes lactic acid to maintain the proper pH.

- Water removes excess heat generated during exercise via the blood.

- Blood volume helps maintain efficient cardiovascular function.

Water loss also reduces the athletes performance potential, sometimes dramatically. Even minimal amounts of water loss impair performance. Studies show that even in short events, dehydration is significant; an athlete who can run a 10,000 meter race in 35 minutes when normally hydrated, will take almost 38 minutes when dehydrated by 4%. An athlete who is well hydrated performing at 100% will diminish performance by 10% if they are only 2% dehydrated. If 5% dehydrated, the athlete's performance will diminish by 30%. This latter example can mean an extra 3 hours or more in an Ironman race!

In conjunction with performance changes with dehydration comes higher heart rates. Four hours of training without water may cause the heart rate to increase by 30 beats.

Comparing the total water loss during rest to competition, water needs increase 10-15 times. In races such as the Japan Ironman, the amount of water lost by an average individual can be as much as 1.5 to 2.5 liters per hour!

It becomes obvious that water needs increase during exercise and especially with competition. How can we compensate for such dramatic losses in water, especially during competition?

The sensation of thirst, regulated by the area of the brain called the hypothalamus, occurs due to the lower concentration of water in the blood. So when you feel thirsty, you're already dehydrated. With most athletes, this delays the intake of water. Following heavy sweating, complete water replacement may take 24 to 48 hours.

So thirst is not a good indication that we need water because that need exists long before we feel thirsty. Unfortunately, the human body does not function like many other animals (by drinking enough water they can consume 10% of their total body weight within the first few minutes after heavy exercise). We need to drink water in small amounts much more frequently.

The best way to regulate water levels is to drink plain water all day long. Avoid carbonated water as it may cause intestinal distress. And during training and competition, the same is true; smaller amounts on a regular basis throughout the activity is the best way to stay as hydrated as possible. Despite this, most competitors will cross the finish line dehydrated to some degree. In addition to not being able to replenish water fast enough, most athletes physically cannot consume enough water. Forcing water beyond your ability will only result in stomach bloating (from swallowing air) or nausea.

During endurance events, liquids containing carbohydrates and sodium are of great value. But these should be in addition to plain water taken during the event. Consuming carbohydrate is important for immediate energy and to maintain the burning of fats – your most important endurance fuel.

Sodium deficiency is related to dehydration and a major concern in endurance activity. With dehydration comes more than just water deficiency. As exercise intensity and duration increase, the sweating rate also increases and sodium loss is accelerated, with minimal losses of potassium. Low blood sodium, called hyponatremia, can result in general weakness and disorientation, and in extreme cases seizures and coma.

In long events, like the Ironman, too much water intake without sodium may aggravate sodium deficiency. So in those events, taking sodium can be very helpful. That's why many drinks contain sodium.

Since water is the major way the body dissipates heat, with dehydration and sodium loss comes the risk of heat illness. Even short races in hot weather can cause heat illness. With heat illness, three stages are seen: muscle cramps, exhaustion and heat stroke.

Muscle cramping, sometimes quite severe, is a classic end result of dehydration. It first attacks the larger, most often used muscles such as the hamstring and quadriceps group, and the calf muscles. Some of the cramping may also be due to sodium deficiency.

The second stage of heat exhaustion is first accompanied by excess fatigue, dizziness, and shortness of breath. Later symptoms include vomiting and fainting. Dehydration causes the cardiovascular system to become inefficient. During this stage of heat illness, blood flow to both the muscles and skin is diminished; the muscles become deficient in nutrients and body heat accumulates.

The last stage of heat illness is heat stroke. This is a life threatening disorder that requires immediate medical attention. The signs include a high internal body temperature (40 degrees C), cessation of sweating, very rapid pulse and breathing, hot and dry skin, confusion and often unconsciousness. If unattended, heat stroke can progress to coma and death. First aid treatment includes cooling the body with cold water or ice.

What should you do to prevent dehydration? Here are some general everyday guidelines:

1. Don't wait for a race to start hydrating. Drink water everyday, throughout the day, especially the week before an event. Drink smaller amounts all day rather than two or three large doses.

2. Have a water bottle near you at all times, and get into the habit of drinking water. Especially keep water near your immediate area during work hours (at your desk, by the phone, etc.) or where you spend much of your time.

3. Consume sodium rich foods (vegetables, sea salt and soy sauce) regularly, especially during hot weather and the week before an event.

4. Get used to drinking water before, during and immediately after training. Simulate race conditions to practice drinking water during faster paces. Learn to drink without swallowing air.

5. Discover which drinks (those with carbohydrates and sodium) make you feel the best and are well tolerated. Experiment during training rather than during a race.

Appendix A: References

The references below are a partial list of many of the small pieces of information used to help integrate both the art and science of my training philosophy. Ultimately, it is up to you as an individual to put all the pieces together to form your own personal, optimal training program.

General Reading

Fats & Oils by Udo Erasmus, Alive Books, Vancouver, Br Columbia. 1986.

Fit or Fat by Covert Bailey. Houghton Mifflin Company, Boston, MA 1978.

Health at the Crossroads by Dean Black, Ph.D. Tapestry Press, Springville, UT 1988.

In Fitness and in Health by Philip Maffetone. David Barmore Productions, Stamford, NY 1994.

Weathering by Stephen Rosen. New York: M Evans and Co, 1979.

Running With Lydiard by Arthur Lydiard. Hodder and Stoughton, Auckland, New Zealand 1983.

The Stress of Life by Hans Selye. McGraw-Hill, New York 1978.

Textbooks

Guyton, AC: *Textbook of Medical Physiology*. WB Saunders, Philadelphia, PA, 1986.

McArdle, WD; Katch, FI and Katch, VL: *Exercise Physiology*. 3rd ed, Lea & Febiger, Philadelphia, PA, 1991.

Murry, RK; Granner, DK; Mayes, PA and Rodwell, VW: *Harper's Biochemistry*. 23rd ed, Appleton & Lange, Norwich CT, 1993.

Walther, DS, *Applied Kinesiology Synopsis*. Systems, DC, Pueblo, CO, 1988.

Wilmore, JH and Costill, DL: *Physiology of Sport and Exercise*. Human Kinetics, Champaign, IL, 1994.

Science Journal Papers

Agre, JC *Hamstring injuries: Proposed etiological factors, prevention, treatment.* Sports Med 2:21-33, 1982.

Banwell, BF, et al: A comparison of aerobic vs. flexibility training in rheumatoid arthritis, abstracted. Arthritis Rheum; 27:S130, 1984

Baycroft, CM and Culp, V. *Running shoes: design facts and functional fantasies.* Chiro Sports Med, Vol 7, No 3, 1993.

Bjorntorp, P. *Importance of fat as a support nutrient for energy.* J Sp Sci, 9 Spec No:71-6, 1991

Brody, DM *Running injuries.* Clinical Symposia, 39(3), 1-36, 1987.

Buroker, KC, and Schwane, JA. *Does post-exercise stretching alleviate delayed muscle soreness?* Phys Sportsmed, 17:65, 1989.

Carter, JE et al. *Fluid replacement during and after exercise in the heat.* Med Sci Sp Exerc, 21:532, 1989.

Cohen, ME et al. *Blood lactate response during moderate exercise in neurocirculatory asthenia, anxiety neurosis, or effort syndrome.* J Clin Invest: 339-342, 1947.

Conconi, F et al. *Determination of the anaerobic threshold by a noninvasive field test in runners.* Cattedra di Biochemica Applicata. Ferrera, Italy, 1980.

Coole, WG, et al. *An analysis of hamstring strains and their rehabilitation.* J.Orthop Sports Phys Ther 9(2), 77-85, 1987.

Costill, DL et al. *Effects of elevated plasma free fatty acids and insulin on muscle glycogen usage during exercise.* J App Phys 43, 695-9, 1977.

Costill, D; King, D; Thomas, R and Hargreaves, M: *Effects of reduced training on muscular power in swimmers.* Phys and Sp Med, 13(2), 94-101, 1985.

Dimsdale, JE and Moss, J. *Plasma Catecholamines in Stress and Exercise.* J Am Med Assoc. 340-342, 1980.

Dintiman, GB *Effects of various training programs on running speed.* Res Q 35,456-463, 1964.

Executive Fitness Newsletter, *A surgeon's warning: Don't do these stretches*, Rodale Press, Emmaus, PA. 1982.

Fuh, MD et al. *Abnormalities of carbohydrate and lipid metabolism in patients with hypertension.* Arch Intern Med 147, 1035-1038, 1987.

Gamow, RI, *Hyperbaric mountain bag instruction manual.* Boulder, CO:1988.

Gardner, LI, et al. *Prevention of lower extremity stress fractures: a controlled trial of a shock absorbent insole.* AJPH 79:12, 1988.

Goldfarb, A. *Antioxidants: role of supplementation to prevent exercise-induced oxidative stress.* Med Sci Sp Exer. Vol. 25:232-236, 1993.

Gollnick, PD and Hermansen, L. *Biochemical adaptations to exercise: Anaerobic metabolism*, Volume I. Academic Press, New York, 1973.

Gorman, JM et al. *Panic disorder and agoraphobia.* In: American Medical Psychiatric Association, Diagnostic and Statistical Manual of Mental Disorders, Third Edition, Washington, DC, 1980.

Grimby, G et al. *Cardiac output during submaximal and maximal exercise in active middle-aged athletes.* J Appl Phys, 21:1150, 1966.

Halbertsma, JP. *Stretching exercises: effect on passive extensibility and stiffness in short hamstrings of healthy subjects.* Arch Phys Med Rehabil Sep;75(9):976, 1994.

Hennerman, E *Relations between structure and function in the design of skeletal muscles.* J. Neurophysiology. 28:581, 1985.

Hickson, R; Foster, C; Pollock, M; Galassi, T and Rich, S: *Reduced training intensities and loss of aerobic power, endurance and cardiac growth.* J Appl Physiol, 58, 492-499, 1985.

Holloszy, J, et al. *Adaptations of skeletal muscle to endurance exercise and their metabolic consequences.* J Appl Physiol, 56, 831-838, 1984.

Hopkins, S., and McKenzie, D. *Hypoxic ventilatory response and arterial desaturation during heavy work.* J. Appl Physiol 67:1119, 1989.

Houmard, J; Costill, D; Mitchell, J; Park, S; Hickner, R and Roemmish, J: *Reduced training maintains performance in distance runners.* Inter J Sports Med, 11, 46-51, 1990.

Howell, DW *Musculoskeletal profile and incidence of musculoskeletal injuries in lightweight women rowers.* Am J Sp Med 12(4), 278-282, 1984.

Iashvilli, AV *Active and passive flexibility in athletes specializing in different sports.* Teority i Praktika Fizicheskoi Kultury 7, 51-52, 1987.

Jenkins, R, et al. *Influence of exercise on clearance of oxidant stress products and loosely bound iron.* Med Sci Sp Exer. Vol. 25:213-17, 1993.

Lafortune, MA, Maguire, KF. *Impact loading of the lower limbs during locomotive activities.* Paper delivered at the 23rd FIMS World Congress of Sports Medicine, Sept. 20-29, 1986, Brisbane, Australia.

Leach, RE. *The prevention and rehabilitation of soft tissue injuries.* Int J. Sports Med 3:18-20, 1982.

Leaf, DA et al. *Respiratory exchange ratio slope: A new concept in the determination of physical fitness and exercise training.* Ann Sp Med, 3:210-214, 1988.

Leisman, G, et al.*Electromyographic effects of fatigue and task repetition on the validity of strong and weak muscle estimates in applied kinesiology muscle testing procedures.* Perceptual and Motor Skills, 80, 933-946, 1995.

Leisman, G, et al. *Somatosensory evoked potential changes during muscle testing.* International Journal of Neuroscience, 45:143-151, 1989.

Linnarsson, D, et al. *Muscle metabolites and oxygen deficit with exercise in hypoxia and hyperoxia.* J Appl Physio. 36:399-402, 1974.

Mostardi, R; Gandee, R and Campbell, T: *Multiple daily training and improvement in aerobic power.* Med and Science in Sports, 7, 82, 1975.

Murphy, DR *A critical look at static stretching: Are we doing our patients harm?* Chiro Sp Med 5(3) 7-70, 1991.

Nose, H et al. *Role of osmolality and plasma volume during rehydration in humans.* J Appl Physiol, 65:325, 1988.

O'Neill, DB *Preventing injuries in young athletes.* J Musculoskel Med 6(11), 21-35, 1989.

Oscal, LB. *Exercise and lipid metabolism.* Prog in Clin & Biological Research. 67:383-390, 1981.

Paffenbarger, RS, et al. *Physical activity, all-cause mortality, and longevity of college alumni.* New England J Med 314:605-613, 1986.

Pitts, FN. *Lactate metabolism in anxiety neurosis.* New Eng J Medicine: 1329-1336, 1967.

Reaven, GM *Role of insulin resistance in human disease.* Diabetes, 37, 1595-1607, 1988.

Robbins, SE, and Hanna, AM. *Running-related injury prevention throught barefoot adaptations.* Med Science in Sports and Exercise, 19:2, 1987.

Simoneau, J, et al. *Human skeletal muscle fiber type alteration with high intensity intermittent training.* Eur J Appl Physiol, 54, 250-253, 1985.

Starcoff, A and Kaelin, X. *Pronation and sports shoe design.* In BM Nigg and BA Kerr, eds. *Biomechanical aspects of sports shoes and playing surfaces.* Calgary, Alberta. University of Calgary, 1983.

Tarnopolsky, L; MacDougal, J; Atkinson, S; Tarnopolsky, M and Sutton, J: *Gender differences in substrate for endurance exercise.* J. Appl Physiol, 68:302, 1990.

Turnstall-Pedoe, D: *Exercise and sudden death.* Br J Sp Med 12:215, 1979.

Van Mechelen, W, et al. *Prevention of running injuries by warm up, cool down and stretching exercises.* Am J Sp Med, 21:711, 1993.

Watt, E; Buskirk, E and Plotnicki, B. *A comparison of single versus multiple daily training regimens: Some physiological considerations.* Research Quarterly, 44, 119-123, 1973.

Williams, J. *Hemoglobin desaturation in highly trained athletes during heavy exercise.* Med Sci Sports Exerc, 18:168, 1986.

Wyndam, CH, et al. *Physiological effects of acute changes in altitude in a deep mine.* J Appl Physio. 36: 399-402, 1974.

Appendix B

The following editorial was written in 1988, in Seoul, South Korea. It was rejected for publication by more than a dozen magazines and newspapers. Some editors responded by saying it was "too unpatriotic," and many others were simply angry and refused to publish such "negativity."

U.S. Athletes: Fit But Unhealthy?

The Games of the XXIV Olympiad in Seoul, South Korea, provided me with a first hand look at the world's great athletes. I also witnessed the continued downfall of the former American dominance.

In 1896, Greece dominated the first Olympic Games by winning the most medals – 47 – but this year in Seoul they managed but a single one. As so often happens in sport, the winners have no place to go but down, as "the losers now will be later to win." Bob Dylan's words have echoed over America for the last couple of decades, and so too have the former foreign losers been winning over American athletes.

The steady decline of American athletic dominance has been slow enough that hardly anyone seems to be noticing, except for the rest of the world. The Soviets, Chinese and Germans, for example, are among many countries who have progressively developed more and more champions. This is not to say that American athletes have not been progressing among themselves. Although they may still break their own records, American athletes have not kept pace with the rest of the world.

When Bryant Gumble told a world T.V. audience that the U.S. athletes were not as good as the '84 team, and not as talented as the Soviets, NBC boldly predicted the obvious. By noon Sunday, the first medals were presented: gold and bronze to the Soviets, and silver to the East Germans. The stage was now set, and the Games continued with that same pace. These Olympics would be the worst showing in history for the U.S.

The glaring problem plaguing U.S. athletes is their lack of health inside an otherwise fit body. This fitness/health imbalance is so common it's often thought to be a normal aspect of athletics. Unfortunately, it prevents some of our best performers from ever reaching the Games while other countries more often send their best.

How do we define fitness and health? Fitness infers athletic ability. The first place finisher is more fit than the runner-up. Health is a state where all the systems of the body – digestive, nervous, circulatory, hormonal, etc. – are working optimally. American athletes are knowingly and unknowingly sacrificing their health for more fitness. Too often they are injured, ill and occasionally even die in the course of their active careers. Both fitness and health should be balanced. The causes are many: diet and nutritional imbalances, over training, improper care, and even attitude.

Attitude problems are more common in U.S. athletes: hoping and believing that a lot of luck is required for a gold medal, and "waking up on the right side of the bed," as silver medalist Michelle Mitchell said, is common. This produces overwhelming stress from competition unlike that seen in most foreign athletes. "Competition makes me happy" said Chinese diver Xu Yanmei, after beating Mitchell for the gold.

This excess competitive stress can, in an unhealthy athlete, cause harm before and during competition, affecting the results. In the previous winter Games in Calgary, U.S. skater Debi Thomas's unsuccessful bid for a gold is one such example. Thomas was unable to perform even near her best due to stress, loosing a seemingly easy gold medal. And in Seoul many foreign swimmers performed a personal best, while most Americans left theirs at the trials weeks earlier.

U.S. athletes and coaches, in their search for the reasons why foreign athletes are over running international events, often cite the drug and "professional athlete" issue, and money problems as causes for the U.S. decline. But our athletes are as capable as any population in the world, and have as much opportunity, if not more, than anyone. The financial concern was best exemplified in the Calgary Games: the U.S. ski team spent 21 million dollars without producing a final-round qualifier, whereas all the medal winning countries combined spent less money.

A more serious money problem, one which effects the health of our future Olympians, comes from the very companies who are "official" sponsors of the U.S. Olympic Team. Many of these companies sell unhealthy products, such as candy bars, colas and alcohol, and spend many millions to advertise their products to, among others, young Olympic hopefuls. And even though the U.S. Olympic Committee does not endorse these products as healthy, our nations young are more naive and view these products as "foods of champions."

The dwindling of our champions is the result of numerous other factors as well. Perhaps the most damaging one is the emphasis of "no pain, no gain." This insistence on quantity, where more is thought to be better, rather quality, where both health and fitness are considered, has unfortunately been a mainstream of American sports for decades.

With an emphasis on building health, and not just bodies, American athletes could minimize injuries, increase their careers and perform at higher levels. As much as any American, I would like to see our athletes perform as they should; "as good as gold." We can begin re-establishing our athletic dominance by the 1996 Games, however it may not happen because of the strong traditional unhealthy trends maintained.

The unwillingness of many to break this tradition is another problem, as more and more countries progress farther ahead of the U.S. in many training and therapeutic abilities. It may be the Asians, led by Japan, China and Korea, who will be the dominant athletic force of the near future, as "the times they are a changing."

Index

About the Author

Dr. Philip Maffetone is an applied kinesiologist and has been in private practice since 1977. An authority on alternative medicine with an extensive background in biochemistry and exercise physiology, certified in Meridian Therapy (acupuncture) and Physiotherapy, Dr. Maffetone also holds a BS degree in human biology and a Doctorate in chiropractic. He has treated and trained many national and world class athletes in almost every sport throughout the world. Some of the champions who have consulted him have included marathoners Priscilla Welch and Lorraine Moller, triathletes Mark Allen, Wendy Ingraham, Donna Peters and Mike Pigg, world champion ultra-marathoner Stu Mittleman and many others. Most importantly, Dr. Maffetone has worked with the so-called middle-of-the-pack athlete who strives toward improved health and fitness.

Dr. Maffetone writes and lectures extensively on human performance throughout the world, including programs for doctors and therapists, and corporate seminars. He is the Past Chairman of the International College of Applied Kinesiology.

Order Form

Please send me:

Training for Endurance by Dr. Philip Maffetone

___ copies at $12.95 plus $4 per book shipping/handling.

In Fitness and in Health by Dr. Philip Maffetone

___ copies at $14.95 plus $4 per book shipping/handling.

*Orders outside North America: Add $8 per book shipping/handling.
**New York residents add 7.25% sales tax.

For fast credit card orders, fax a copy of this page to 607-652-7610

Name: _____

Address: _____

_____

City: _____ State: _____ Zip: _____

Enclosed is my ☐ check ☐ money order for $ _____

DO NOT SEND CASH

Charge my: ☐ Master Card ☐ Visa

Card # _____

Exp. date _____

Signature _____

Mail To:

David Barmore Productions
P.O. Box 250
Stamford, NY 12167
607-652-7610